French Household Cooking

'In the interests of home life, a well-cooked dinner is of more importance than a well-dressed wife. A man will admire a pretty dress, but in time he will get used to the unsatisfactory result of clothes; he never gets tired of good food dressed with care and taste' writes the author of *French Household Cookery*. Frances Keyzer was an Englishwoman who lived in Paris at the beginning of the twentieth century, when French women were reckoned to be the cleverest of cooks, and the Parisians the cleverest of all. Imagination, economy and simplicity were the hallmarks of French domestic cookery, the latter particularly attractive to English women at a time when the lack of servants meant that many women were having to cook themselves for the first time. Feminine independence was also on the rise, producing women of the world with less time to spend in the kitchen. Intended to be an aid to these women, *French Household Cookery* begins with the elementary rules of good cooking – cleanliness, fresh ingredients and good butter – and goes on to present a hundred and thirty-seven recipes for well-loved domestic dishes that rely upon the simple methods employed in French homes, where daily meals were always as well prepared as at the most luxurious tables. There are nineteen chapters, beginning with *hors-d'oeuvres* and ending with a chapter on menus and recipes from chefs of the best Paris restaurants, including the fabled Ledoyen and Marguery's, where the same emphasis on fresh ingredients, careful cooking and attractive presentation are seen. Men are not the only beneficiaries of good cooking. As the author notes – '*A French philosopher and observer of men and women in the highest classes of society has made a study of the effects of good living upon the fair sex. He concluded that carefully prepared food has been proved to give brilliance to the eyes, freshness to the skin, strength to the muscles and it can safely be said that women who know what to eat are comparatively ten years younger than those who ignore the science*'.

T0347953

French Household Cooking

Cooking

With Recipes From The Best Chefs Of Paris

Frances Keyzer

Routledge
Taylor & Francis Group
LONDON AND NEW YORK

First published 2006 by Kegan Paul

Published 2013 by Routledge
2 Park Square, Milton Park, Abingdon, Oxfordshire OX14 4RN
711 Third Avenue, New York, NY 10017, USA

First issued in paperback 2016

Routledge is an imprint of the Taylor & Francis Group, an informa business

British Library Cataloguing in Publication Data

Keyzer, Frances
French household cooking: with recipes from the best chefs of Paris. - (Library of
culinary arts)
1. Cookery, French
I. Title
641.5'944

ISBN 13: 978-1-138-97465-4 (pbk)
ISBN 13: 978-0-7103-1079-8 (hbk)

PREFACE TO THE SIXTH EDITION

CONDITIONS to-day have altered the French view of housekeeping. It is a recognised fact that no women on the face of the globe are as clever, where the question of food is concerned, as the French; and, in truth, to put it colloquially, the Parisienne takes the cake.

With the remains of cold meat—the bugbear of the British cook—she makes a succulent stew, where even the most knowing are nonplussed. With a few onions, a couple of tomatoes and a spoonful of curry powder, meat, fish, and fowl are metamorphosed.

Can anything be more useful, at present, than to learn how this is done?

To start with, it is an undisputed fact that feeding has become simpler; and, where at one time a four or five course dinner was considered essential to smartness, to-day, in the best houses, a dish of fish and fowl are all that one requires. Sweets are replaced by cheese and a bowl of fruit.

White table-cloths have almost disappeared in favour of a slip of lace or Chinese embroidery, or even of coloured cloths, and economy is thus effected in the washing bill. The popular dishes are those which require very little butter and no eggs. In this revised edition a chapter on economical dishes has been added, and some useful recipes are included. It cannot be said that the viands have improved in flavour, but they suit the temperament of the hour. A case in point is the making of pancakes without eggs which will be explained in this revised edition.

But a factor in French cooking is, undoubtedly, the patent stewing-pot. It is wonderful in its labour-saving properties and gives the housewife time to attend to the necessary requirements of the household while the dinner cooks itself. This pot is filled with water; beef and bones, carrots, turnips, onions, salt and pepper are added; and, hermetically closed, it can simmer for hours when once brought to boiling-point, without danger of spoiling the contents. A quarter of an hour is said to be all that is necessary to make meat and vegetables palatable, but the well-advised give the quarter of an hour at full speed and leave the saucepan on the corner of the stove for the contents to simmer gently until required.

A broth, a meat course, and a dish of vegetables result.

In old-fashioned families this stewing-pot is taboo because the lid cannot be lifted to scent the flavour; but old-fashioned families are disappearing, and the pot remains.

Celery makes three dishes to-day in the hands of experienced Frenchwomen. They start by extracting the full aroma in soup. Then some of the vegetable is removed, covered with a white sauce, and served as a course. The remaining branches are cut in pieces and mixed with a mayonnaise. The soup and vegetable are served at one meal, the salad at another.

The French cook, in fact, is up-to-date.

THE DAILY MEALS WITHOUT SERVANTS

It is an undisputed fact that we have learnt to do without them, as the song says. In fact, the lack of servants has made women more independent and has brought forth a number of inventions that would have astonished our grandmothers.

To begin with, we have the patent saucepans which have already been described. Every country has some patent that is supposed to be better than others, but this patent saucepan is undoubtedly an excellent invention, as it saves both time and labour.

The family dish consists of a piece of beef—half bone, half meat—water, salt and pepper, and a handful of onions, carrots, turnips, and leeks. The broth makes a nutritious soup, the beef and vegetables (with boiled potatoes added) are excellent served with, or without, a tomato sauce.

With the remains of the beef a number of preparations are made that can be varied each day.

The favourite ways are as follows:

The beef cut in cubes; the same quantity of potatoes, butter or margarine, tomato sauce. The potatoes are browned slightly in the pan where the butter or margarine has been heated; the beef is added, and the sauce follows in due course.

Another way is to add an equal quantity of sausage meat, mutton or veal; twice the quantity of boiled rice (or bread moistened with milk) or mashed potatoes, parsley, salt and pepper. Chop the meat, mix with the rice, bread or potatoes, and butter a dish that can stand the oven; pour in the preparation and bake for twenty minutes.

A third is to mix chopped onions with the chopped beef and place in a dish beneath a thick layer of mashed potatoes. Heat in the oven.

LABOUR-SAVING UTENSILS

Of all the inventions that have appeared of late for labour-saving in the kitchen, there is nothing to equal the "fifteen-minutes" saucepans. The majority of house-keepers are trying them with good results, and time saved is valuable. Whether the cooking is as perfect as in former days is another matter. But, time gained is everything at present with the price of fuel, gas, and electricity.

Another invention is Pyrex, that remarkable glass ware that we cook in and send to table. For macaroni, "soufflés," eggs, all dishes *au gratin*, it is like the Waverley pen, a boon and a blessing to men . . . and women too.

F. K.

CONTENTS

INDEX

Index

A Special Index will be found on pp. 126-128. It contains a number of recipes conveniently classified under separate headings :

> Quickly Prepared Dishes.
> Small Family Dishes.
> Dishes for a Dinner Party.
> Dishes Suitable for Beginners.
> Dishes Suitable for Servantless Houses.
> Cold Meals.

INTRODUCTION

" Animals feed, men eat, but only intelligent men know what to eat."—BRILLAT-SAVARIN.

THIS Cookery Book is not meant to take the place of the hundred and more thick volumes that have been compiled within the last fifty years. It neither pretends to explain the various terms in use among the chefs of the haute cuisine, nor to indicate the innumerable ways of preparing fish, flesh, or fowl that every professed cook knows as well or better than most writers on the subject. It is intended to give a few suggestions to women of the world who appreciate the advantages of well-prepared food, and know the value that such food has in married life.

A series of well-chosen, well-cooked dinners, not necessarily large ones, will attract a man and keep him at home —interested and amiable—more than the ordinary woman supposes. In the interests of home life a well-cooked dinner is of more importance than a well-dressed wife. A man will admire a pretty dress, but in time he will get used to the unsatisfactory result of clothes; he never gets tired of good food, dressed with care and taste.

This book is therefore not intended as a complete Cours de Cuisine, but as an aid to women, and an indication of the simple methods employed in French homes, where the daily meals are always well prepared, at the humblest as at the most luxurious tables.

The elementary rules of good cooking are cleanliness, fresh ingredients, and good butter. The quality of the butter used in the preparing of eggs, vegetables, fish, meat, and sauces is of the greatest importance. In fact, in this matter alone is the secret of the different flavour of a plain dish cooked at the good restaurant from the same cooked at the " wine shop at the corner." A dish of French beans, small and tender, will be prepared in the same manner by the proprietor of the shop as by the chef at the restaurant; but one will use " kitchen " butter, the other will employ the finest to be procured.

In French household cooking, good fresh butter is always used.

Another important factor is the utensil. Saucepans and frying-pans play a great part in the cooking of food. They must be scrupulously clean, and as the ordinary cook is more or less careless in this respect, the utensils should be either in common red earthenware or in china.

With half a dozen china saucepans of all sizes, a couple of frying-pans, an earthenware pot for soup, a smaller one for vegetables, a " cocotte " (a cast-iron stew-pan and cover), and a fish-kettle, the average household is ready for all emergencies.

In this volume recipes will be given for dishes prepared in French households. They comprise the ordinary, inexpensive preparations of fresh food, with such ingredients as are at the command of moderate incomes. The object, in fact, is to show the simplicity and excellence of the French methods of dealing with articles of food, retaining their nutritive properties, and making them palatable and digestible as well as presentable.

The decoration of dishes from a purely decorative point of view is not practised here; every artichoke, carrot, or turnip that surrounds a piece of meat is not only cut into an appetising shape, but is flavoured in an appetising manner. The French are not satisfied with something pleasing to the eye; it must also be pleasing to the taste.

A French philosopher and observer of men and women in the highest classes of Society has made a study of the effects of good living upon the fair sex. " Succulent, delicate, and carefully prepared food has been proved by a series of minute studies to delay the exterior signs of age. It gives brilliance to the eyes, freshness to the skin, strength to the muscles, and as it is acknowledged that the depression of the muscles causes wrinkles, it can safely be said that all women who know what to eat are comparatively ten years younger than those who ignore this science."

With this reasoning, joined to the pleasure of contenting the breadwinner, there is no excuse for women to despise the material question of food. A youthful-looking wife and a well-cooked dinner will make a happy home.

F. K.

French Household Cooking

CHAPTER I

HORS-D'ŒUVRE

THE hors-d'œuvre are little light dishes that have the double advantage of decorating a luncheon table and stimulating the appetite. A good assortment of hors-d'œuvre is a pleasant introduction to a meal. While the guests are partaking of one and another of these cold dishes there is ample time to prepare the first warm dish, which is better appreciated after the expectant prelude.

For a simple luncheon two or three hors-d'œuvre suffice; but when there are three or four courses the hors-d'œuvre are more numerous.

They comprise:

Radishes.—These are thrown into a basin full of water, well washed, and all the leaves removed but one or two of the small green ones. They are placed in a small oblong dish arranged with the little green leaves forming the border.

Butter.—Arranged in a separate dish in little balls, or any fancy design, ornamented with a spray of parsley.

Anchovies.—Scraped, washed, and filleted, served with slices of hard eggs, covered with chopped parsley.

Sardines.—Tunnyfish.

Eggs in Jelly.
Eggs in Mayonnaise. } Explained in Chapter XIII.

Peeled Shrimps in Mayonnaise.

Slices of Bologna or Spiced Sausage.

Slices of Smoked Salmon.

Caviare on Toast, served with lemon.

Olives.—French or Spanish are the most favoured.

Epicures have discovered that one or two unconventional hors-d'œuvre give the guest a foretaste of the nature of the meal that is to follow. It is therefore as necessary to concoct something unusual in the hors-d'œuvre as to vary the table decorations. Here are a couple of " preludes," as we will call them, that are generally much appreciated.

Shredded Celeriac.

The root is scraped, washed, and cut into the thinnest of strips, like straws, about an inch long, and covered with a mayonnaise into which a large spoonful of mustard has been incorporated. The strips are mixed with the mayonnaise, with the help of a spoon and fork, until every particle is covered with the thick sauce.

Potatoes and Shrimps.

The smallest potatoes are selected for this hors-d'œuvre, as when cut into small rounds they make a prettier dish than the larger potato.

Boil the necessary quantity in their skins. When cooked, peel them, and cut them into little round slices the thickness of a key-ring. Let them cool in a little oil and vinegar. Peel a good number of shrimps, almost as many as there are slices of potato; remove the potatoes from the oil and vinegar, throw them with the shrimps into a small dish, and mix well with the mayonnaise, which must be highly seasoned with salt and pepper.

CHAPTER II

In France the national soups are the pot-au-feu or clear soup made from beef, and vegetable soups made without any meat or meat stock whatever. There are, of course, a number of variants of the meat soup, as far as the thickening properties are concerned, such as Italian paste, tapioca, etc.; but the fundamental meat soup is the clear bouillon that is so little understood outside France.

Pot-au-feu (*Clear Meat Soup*).

Every French kitchen, from the poorest to the richest, contains a large earthenware pot with a cover, for the making of the indispensable pot-au-feu. In some households the meat from which the soup is made is eaten in the kitchen, in others it forms part of the daily menu. There can be no rules where taste plays the all-important part. Some people have not considered they have dined unless a piece of boiled beef follows the soup; others never eat beef on any occasion, boiled or otherwise.

For the family pot-au-feu, which consists of clear soup, followed by the beef and vegetables cooked therein, the juiciest and most serviceable piece of meat for making good soup where the beef can be eaten and enjoyed is the " paleron " or shoulder of beef. It is customary to make sufficient soup for two repasts. The pot is filled with cold water, a handful of " kitchen " salt thrown in, and about three or four pounds of beef (according to the number of people to eat it). The pot is placed on a quick fire, and when the water boils it is immediately skimmed. The skimming process may take from ten minutes to a quarter of an hour, but it is indispensable for the clearness of the soup. When this operation is effected the soup must no longer boil quickly, but just simmer gently on the corner of

3

the stove, or on a gas fire at its lowest lighting power, for five or six hours.   Two or three carrots, turnips, and leeks are added, and no more attention is given to the pot-au-feu (except to see it has not ceased simmering) until about half an hour before serving, when, if convenient, the giblets of a fowl are washed and added, giving the soup a more delicate flavour, and improving the bouillon materially.

The important moment of removing the fat from the surface of the soup has now arrived, and this is effected with great care.   A sufficient quantity of soup is then ladled into a saucepan, allowed to boil, coloured slightly with a few drops of the ordinary colouring matter or a little burnt sugar, and thickened with tapioca or vermicelli; or simply poured into the soup tureen over round slices of bread fried in butter.

The meat and vegetables are taken from the large pot and served up, the meat being in the centre of the dish; the carrots, turnips, and leeks around it without any gravy or water.

The remainder of the soup is kept for the next day; and the beef—if there should be any—is warmed in the soup, and served, cut into rather thick slices, covered with a tomato or piquante sauce.

The muddy nature of the ordinary English cooked soup has two causes: the first, that it is not sufficiently skimmed; the second, that it boils too quickly.   If these simple suggestions are attended to, there is no reason why the most inexperienced cook should not make a clear soup or bouillon.

Bouillon aux Œufs pochés (Clear Soup with Poached Eggs).

When the fat has been removed from the soup, the necessary quantity for a large or small family is boiled in a saucepan, and coloured, salted, and peppered to taste. In the meanwhile an egg for each person is poached and placed in the soup tureen, and the hot soup poured carefully over them.   When serving, one egg is ladled into each plate.

Potage Parmentier (Potato Soup).

This very simple family soup is excellent, if prepared carefully, and has the advantage of being both inexpensive and quickly made. The ingredients are the white portion of two or three leeks, according to the size; three or four potatoes; a little chervil; butter; a cup of boiled milk, or half a cupful of cream; and a few cubes of fried bread. The leeks must be cut down the centre to facilitate the cleansing of this somewhat sandy vegetable, and thrown into a basin of cold water. The potatoes are peeled. A saucepan is set on the fire with a small piece of butter in it about the size of a walnut; the leeks are cut into pieces and thrown into the saucepan, and allowed to cook uncovered on a slow fire for about seven or eight minutes. Then a little over a quart of water is added, with salt to taste, and the potatoes. In about twenty minutes leeks and potatoes will be cooked; they are then placed in a strainer, and pressed with a wooden pestle to reduce them to a purée; the water from which they were taken is brought to the boil again and the purée poured back into it, the whole being constantly stirred with a wooden spoon. Then a handful of cubes of bread are browned in a frying-pan with a little butter, and are placed in the soup tureen, together with the milk or cream, a lump of butter about the size of a large egg, and a pinch of chervil leaves without a particle of stalk. The contents of the saucepan are now poured gently into the tureen, the wooden spoon is again brought into action, as the stirring process is always necessary when a hot liquid comes in contact with butter, salt and a little pepper are added, and the soup is ready.

These quantities are given for five or six persons; for a larger number it is only necessary to add more leeks, more potatoes, and more butter. The flavour will depend on the quality of the butter, the salt, and the pepper, and the delicacy of the soup upon the use of milk or cream. Cream in this soup permits of it being called " parmentier " and being placed on a friendly menu; without the cream it becomes the plain potato soup. A few pennyworths of cream make all the difference.

Potage Argenteuil.

This soup takes its name from the water which constitutes its base—water in which the Argenteuil asparagus has been boiled. But asparagus from any other regions is equally good for making a savoury and nutritious soup. Any doctor will tell you that the vegetables we eat lose the greater part of their nourishment in the water; therefore, in order to get the benefit of these nutritive properties, what can be more logical than to drink the water; in other words, make soup of it. The asparagus is cooked in the ordinary way and served as a vegetable; the water is poured into a large saucepan and boiled again. In the meanwhile a cupful of rice is washed, and a handful of sorrel leaves held under running water to cleanse them. A small piece of butter is placed in a saucepan with the sorrel, and stirred to keep it from " catching "; the boiling water from the asparagus is poured into it, and the rice is added, and salted and peppered. In twenty minutes the rice is cooked. The yolk of an egg is beaten in the soup tureen, a lump of butter follows, the contents of the saucepan are stirred gradually into it, and the soup is ready.

Potage Soissons.

This is another popular family soup, made with the water in which white beans have been cooked. A quart of these white beans are soaked overnight, and boiled in a sufficient quantity of water in the usual way, with a handful of salt; they are served as a vegetable, and the water used for soup, which is made in the same manner as the Potage Argenteuil with rice and sorrel. With a portion of the beans added, this soup is very nutritious.

Potage Crème de Chou-fleur (Cauliflower purée).

This is a delicious and delicate soup that can be served at any dinner-party. The ingredients for about a couple of quarts of soup, sufficient for eight or nine people, are a large white cauliflower, a quart of milk, eight tablespoonfuls of tapioca, a piece of butter the size of an egg, the yolks of two eggs, and a small cup of cream, salt, and a pinch of white sugar. The cauliflowers must be selected firm and not too full blown, for when this vegetable is over-ripe the flavour is too strong. The cauliflower must be washed, and each flower broken or cut in order to cleanse it thoroughly, then placed in a saucepan in a quart of cold water with a handful of salt. The saucepan is covered until the water boils; then uncovered until the cauliflower is quite cooked, within a quarter of an hour. The covering and uncovering of the saucepan is necessary in order to prevent the cauliflower from becoming yellow. It is then taken out of the water and passed through a hair sieve to obtain the purée. The water in which it has cooked is now put on the fire again, and when boiling the tapioca is poured into it like " rain," so that the grains do not stick together, brought to boiling-point again, and then removed to the side of the fire to simmer for about twenty minutes. In the meantime the milk is boiled, a pinch of sugar added, and then poured into the tapioca with the purée of cauliflower, turning constantly with a wooden spoon to prevent " catching." Now break the yolks of two eggs into the soup tureen, add the cream and beat them together; add also the butter in small pieces, all in the soup tureen; then slowly pour the contents of the saucepan, almost boiling, into the tureen, turning continually with a wooden spoon. It is essential to pour in a small quantity of the liquid at first, in order to avoid the too rapid cooking of the eggs; if this is not given the requisite attention, the soup will not be smooth and velvety as it should be. This soup is served with a few peas boiled in salt water, or with little cubes of bread fried in butter, to " dress " it.

Potage Cresson (Water-Cress Soup).

Wash two bunches of water-cress; pluck the leaves from the thick stems and throw them into a saucepan of boiling water. After a minute remove the cress with a strainer and chop it finely; put a piece of butter into another saucepan and add the chopped cress; turn it with a spoon in the butter on a slow fire for a few seconds, then add hot water sufficient to make the soup. When it boils, drop in as many tablespoonfuls of tapioca as there are guests; salt and pepper. Beat the yolk of an egg in the soup tureen, add a lump of butter (and a small cup of double cream if convenient), and when the tapioca is cooked, slowly pour the contents of the saucepan into the tureen, stirring constantly in order to avoid curdling the egg. This soup can be made without cream, but is greatly improved if cream is added to the egg and butter.

Potage Bisque (Crayfish Soup).

Boil the écrevisses (crayfish) in white wine and water, with salt, pepper, a few slices of onion, and the usual herbs tied together in the aromatic bouquet, known in culinary parlance as a *bouquet garni*. When cooked remove the tails, pound the bodies with some rice that has boiled in good stock, then pass through a hair sieve, and add stock and a little of the water in which the écrevisses have boiled. Break the yolk of an egg in the soup tureen, beat it, and add a little thick cream and a piece of butter, pour the soup gently into it, turning constantly with a wooden spoon. Throw in the tails of the fish and serve.

Potage Écossais (the French for Scotch Broth)

Cut into small pieces three or four carrots, turnips, leeks, and a head of celery. Put a piece of butter into the saucepan and add the vegetables. When they begin to colour add a sufficient quantity of mutton broth or water; salt and pepper. When boiling add a cupful of pearl barley. In this soup the flavour of the leeks and celery should predominate.

Potage Germiny.

Take a small handful of sorrel, and throw it into a saucepan with a little butter. In a few minutes it is cooked. In the meanwhile boil a small cupful of ground rice in sufficient water to make the soup. Beat the yolks of two eggs in a little cream in the soup tureen; salt and pepper the rice and pour it slowly into the tureen. Add the sorrel just before serving.

Potage Comtesse.

Make a purée of white beans, boiling the beans in water with salt and pepper, and passing them through a sieve. Beat the yolk of an egg and a little cream in the soup tureen, and add the purée of beans and the water in which the beans were cooked.

Potage Alexandre.

Boil a pint of flageolets—green beans—with salt. In another saucepan place a lump of butter and add a good handful of sorrel. Pass the beans through a strainer into the saucepan containing the sorrel, and pour into it sufficient water or stock to make the soup. Beat the yolks of two eggs in the soup tureen, with or without a cup of cream, and pour the contents of the saucepan into the tureen, gently mixing with a wooden spoon.

Potage Sontay.

Boil a pint of lentils and a pint of white beans, pass them through a strainer into another saucepan in a purée. Add the water in which the beans and lentils have cooked, with salt and pepper. When boiling throw in a cupful of boiled rice, and more water if necessary. Put a lump of butter into the tureen and pour in the soup.

Potage Albert.

Boil a pint of white beans and a pint of young scarlet runners, broken into small pieces (not cut). In the same saucepan add a large peeled potato and two tomatoes. When the potatoes and tomatoes are cooked, remove them and work them into a paste in a bowl, with two tablespoonfuls of good salad oil and a little basil if possible. When the amalgamation is complete pour it into the saucepan when the beans are cooked. Add salt and pepper, and serve in the soup tureen.

Specially recommended.

The beans that make the best soup are those that have a large pod and a long thick bean. They are broken into pieces, and both parts thrown into boiling water. The Albert soup is not a purée. Its feature is the combination of green and white beans; the liquid should be a light red, occasioned by the addition of the pounded tomato and potato.

Purée Duboys.

The gourmet who told me how this soup is prepared had tears in his eyes as he remembered how he had looked round to see if there were a second plateful after he had tasted the first spoonful, and the tureen was empty. Be warned and have a large supply.

Ingredients:
One cup of white beans.
One cup of lentils.
One carrot.
One potato.
One teaspoonful of tapioca for each person.
One handful of sorrel.
Salt, pepper, butter.

Steep the dried vegetables in water for a few hours— or more if possible. Put a saucepan on the fire full of cold water; throw in the beans and lentils; salt and pepper. Let them boil until tender. In the meanwhile wash and pluck the sorrel; place a lump of butter in a stew-pan, and when melted throw in the sorrel. Slice the carrot and potato; wash the tapioca and add the carrot and potato to the beans and lentils. When sufficiently cooked, add the sorrel that has been simmering in the butter in the stew-pan; pass the contents of the saucepan through a colander to make a purée—taking care to have a recipient beneath it. Pour everything back into the saucepan; boil again; add a little vinegar if the sorrel is not sharp enough; salt and pepper to taste, and serve.

Potage Napolitain (Tomato Soup).

One pound of ripe tomatoes.
Three large potatoes.
One handful of sorrel.

Wash the tomatoes and sorrel; peel the potatoes. Boil all together in water slightly salted. Pass the vegetables through a fine colander into a bowl or basin; put them again into the water in which they were cooked, with a lump of butter, a piece of sugar, and some salt. Fry some cubes of bread in butter, throw them into the soup tureen, and pour the soup over them when it has boiled for a few minutes.

Potage Milanais (Tomato Soup).

One pound of ripe tomatoes are boiled in water with a handful of salt, passed through a colander with a wooden spoon to make them into a purée, and poured back again into the water. When the soup boils again, as many spoonfuls of tapioca or vermicelli are added as there are guests, with a little pepper. A lump of butter is put into soup tureen and the hot soup poured over it. Sufficient water is put into the saucepan to make the soup.

Another Potato Soup.

Wash four leeks, cut them two or three times lengthways; chop them into small pieces; peel and wash three large potatoes, cut them also into small pieces. Put the leeks and potatoes into a saucepan full of cold water; let it boil; add a handful of salt. After the soup has boiled half an hour add six tablespoonfuls of rice. Boil again for an hour and a quarter. Just before serving add a lump of butter the size of an egg. This soup has a nutty flavour.

Potage Saint-Germain (Pea Soup).

Boil a quart of dried or fresh peas in a quart of water, with a handful of salt. (It is well known that dried vegetables are placed in cold water, and green vegetables in boiling water.) When cooked pass them through a sieve to make a purée, with another saucepan beneath to catch the soup. Throw the purée back again into the same water and let it boil once more. Then add salt and pepper, and a teaspoonful of tapioca for each person. When the tapioca is cooked, place a lump of butter in the soup tureen and a small cupful of cream, and pour the contents of the saucepan slowly into it, stirring constantly with a wooden spoon. The appearance of the soup is improved if a handful of fresh green peas are boiled and thrown into the tureen at the last moment.

Soupe à l'Oignon (Onion Soup).
A Popular and Nutritious Paris Soup.

Place a lump of butter the size of an egg in an earthen saucepan on the fire. When the butter is melted, chop a couple of medium-sized onions and throw them into the hot butter. Stir with a wooden spoon to prevent burning. When a golden brown add sufficient hot water to make the quantity of soup required for four or six people, and a handful of salt. When the water boils, strain the contents of the saucepan through a colander into another vessel and replace the water only in the saucepan to boil again. Add about a quarter of a pound of grated cheese to the boiling soup and a few pieces of toasted or fried bread. Place a small piece of fresh butter in the soup tureen and pour the contents of the saucepan upon it. This soup is sometimes put into the oven for a few minutes to " gratiner," but this is not necessary. It is, however, an improvement.

Vermicelli Soup without Meat.

Place a handful of salt in a saucepan full of hot water upon the fire. When the water boils, put in sufficient vermicelli to make a thick soup. When cooked, break the yolk of an egg into the soup tureen, beat the egg slightly, add a small piece of butter, and pour in the hot vermicelli and water, stirring with a wooden spoon. Grated cheese makes a little change to the taste of this palatable soup.

A Hint to Economical Housekeepers.

All water in which vegetable or meat has been boiled should be used to make soup. Any cold potatoes, rice, dried beans, etc., from the previous day are thrown into the soup, boiled again, and thus utilised.

CHAPTER III

FISH

Fillets of Turbot or Plaice Béarnaise.

Remove the fillets from the bone of the fish, also the skin. Wash them, and dry on a clean cloth; salt and flour each fillet, dip them into egg, then cover with bread-crumbs. Put a piece of butter into a stew-pan, and when the butter steams add the fillets, and brown on both sides. Serve on a long dish with a border of béarnaise sauce, and a béarnaise in a sauce-boat. (See Chapter on Sauces.)

Matelotte à l'Ancienne (a Fish Stew).

Cut a carp and an eel into small pieces. Colour them in butter on a very quick fire. Pour a little brandy into a stew-pan in which they are lying and set light to it. Then add a bottle of red wine (which can be bought quite cheaply in France), a couple of carrots, four onions, and a bouquet of herbs (parsley, thyme, and bay). Boil for a quarter of an hour; then remove the pieces into a dish. Put into a small saucepan a lump of butter and a table-spoonful of flour, work them well together when the butter melts, and pour in the contents of the saucepan where the fish has cooked. Pass this through a fine sieve into a clean saucepan, arrange the pieces in a pyramid, pour the sauce over them, and serve with triangular pieces of fried bread around the dish.

Sole au Gratin (Sole).

Choose a large sole, remove the skin, clean it well so that none of the blood remains inside. If this is not carefully wiped with the cloth it gives a bitter taste to the fish. Place the sole in a dish that can stand the fire.

13

Salt and pepper on both sides; chop two or three shalots and a little parsley, and sprinkle over the sole; add a lump of butter divided into small pieces, a glass of white wine, and a layer of bread-crumbs. Let it cook in the oven, and serve in the same dish. A large plaice may be prepared in the same manner.

Filets de Soles Normande (Sole).

Remove the fillets from the soles. Place them in cold water with the juice of a lemon. Boil the bones of the fish with a carrot, a couple of onions, and a bouquet of herbs. Put a lump of butter into a small saucepan, let it melt and add a tablespoonful of flour; work one into the other, off the fire, with a wooden spoon; moisten with the water which has been boiling with the bones and herbs, and let it boil and thicken for about ten minutes, stirring occasionally. In the meanwhile dry the fillets on a cloth, salt and pepper them, wrap each piece in buttered paper, and cook them in the oven on a buttered dish. Serve the fillets on a long dish, with mussels and peeled shrimps. Add the yolks of two eggs and a small cup of cream to the sauce, and pour it over the fish.

Filets de Sole à la Crème (Soles with Cream).

The fillets are poached in the oven; the bones are boiled as in the preceding recipe. A sauce is made with flour and butter and the fish-water. Cream is added according to the quantity of fillets. Then the fillets are placed in another dish (silver or china); the sauce is poured over them. A little grated Gruyère is sometimes added, and the dish is put into the oven for a few minutes, but not long enough to brown.

Grondins au Blanc (Red Gurnet).

This is a dish of fish that is served cold, and is appreciated in summer. Gurnet is not an expensive fish and is consequently little known to restaurant frequenters under its own name. A large red head and an elongated body are not attractive or conducive to long prices on a menu, but the humble gurnet is delicate eating, and finds its way into many a " timbale " when soles are not plentiful. In Paris a fish of moderate size costs a few halfpence, and a dish for six or eight people is not an extravagant item when it can be made from three or four gurnets.

Select large fish in preference to the smaller ones, and three will make a presentable dish.

Place a saucepan on the fire with cold water, salt in sufficient quantity to taste, pepper, a couple of carrots cut in slices, half a dozen onions and a bunch of thyme, bay, and parsley tied together. In the meantime wash and clean the gurnet and place them in the saucepan as soon as they are ready, and boil for half an hour. Remove them from the water and cut them into pieces about the length of a finger, taking away all bone and skin. Place these pieces on a round dish in pyramid form, covering the centre, of course, and mounting as high as the quantity of fish allows. The object is to make the dish as attractive as possible by raising it in the middle, placing one piece of fish across the other, and so on, until every particle is removed from the bone.

Then make the sauce that is to cover the fish entirely.

In a small saucepan place a piece of butter, a little larger than an egg. Let it melt a little and then add two tablespoonfuls of flour; work them together with a wooden spoon; adding little by little the water from the large saucepan in which the fish has cooked. It is advisable to strain the water before using it for the sauce, but in most households the cook simply ladles out the water from one saucepan into another as she requires it, as the flour and butter thicken, taking care of course to leave the carrots and onions, etc. When there is sufficient sauce made, remove the saucepan from the fire, add the juice of two lemons and the yolks of two eggs, which must be well mixed with the sauce while it is still warm, but not on the fire, so that the eggs do not curdle. The sauce must now be tasted to see if it requires more pepper and salt, the necessary quantity is added, and the sauce, which should be as thick as double cream and sufficiently sour, is now poured all over the fish, placed in a cool larder, and is ready to be served on the following day, the dish garnished with slices of lemon.

Grondins au Citron (Red Gurnet).

The fish is prepared as in the preceding recipe. The sauce is made with three eggs and two lemons and the fish stock. The eggs are broken into a bowl and beaten for a few minutes until well mixed. Salt and pepper are added. The lemons are squeezed, strained, and added to the eggs with about half a pint of the water in which the fish has cooked; then poured into a jug and placed in a saucepan full of boiling water, to thicken as for a custard. When the sauce is as thick as cream it is ready. Bone the fish, and cut it into pieces; throw the sauce over it and serve hot or cold.

Moules Marinières (Mussels).

Mussels are rarely eaten in England, but as soon as a travelled Englishman arrives on the Continent he is certain to ask for " Moules Marinières." Mussels are excellent food if they are caught on the rocks.

Scrape the mussels, wash them in a large basin, then place them in a saucepan on the fire. After a few minutes they will open. Place the shell that contains the mussel into a dish. Prepare the following sauce. Put a piece of butter the size of an egg into a small saucepan. When melted add a tablespoonful of flour; mix well together with a wooden spoon and moisten with a little milk and some of the water in which the mussels have opened. Add chopped parsley, salt and pepper, and pour this sauce over the mussels in the dish. Or make the sauce in a large saucepan, and let the mussels warm therein for a few moments before serving.

Harengs, Sauce moutarde (Herrings).

Clean and wash some fresh herrings; dry them with a cloth and cook them on the grill. Serve with the following sauce. In a small saucepan place a lump of butter, a dessertspoonful of flour, a dash of vinegar, and a table-spoonful of mustard, salt and pepper, and a little water. Mix these ingredients with a wooden spoon upon the fire until they thicken. When the herrings are cooked, remove them to a hot dish, and pour the sauce over them.

Maquereau à la Maître d'hôtel (Mackerel).

Grill the mackerel in the usual manner. Melt a lump of butter in a saucepan with a little chopped parsley and chives, salt and pepper, and the juice of a lemon, and pour it over the fish.

Matelote d'anguilles (Stewed Eels).

Cut a moderate sized eel in pieces, when skinned (an eel weighing a pound is the best for eating), put a little bacon in cubes into a saucepan with a small piece of butter and a sprinkling of flour; when brown add the eel, turn it with a wooden spoon until coloured on all sides. Pour a tablespoonful of brandy into the saucepan and set light to it. Then add a pint of red wine and a pint of water, salt, pepper, bay leaf, thyme, parsley, and a couple of small onions. Cover the saucepan, and let the contents boil gently until the fish is cooked—about half an hour— remove the herbs, and serve surrounded with triangles of fried bread.

Saumon Sauce Verte (Salmon with a Green Sauce).

Put a fish kettle on the fire with water, salt, pepper, an onion, a carrot cut in slices, and bouquet of herbs. Boil a piece of salmon therein. Remove the skin when the salmon is cooked. Make a mayonnaise sauce. Take a handful of spinach, boil it in a little water and squeeze the leaves through a muslin over a bowl. This liquid is added to the mayonnaise, and makes the green sauce that looks so appetising with the pink salmon. The fish can be served either hot or cold.

Homard à l'Américaine (Lobster).

Cut a lobster, alive, into small pieces and cook them in butter in a saucepan. Add a couple of glasses of white wine and a spoonful of purée of tomatoes, salt, pepper, a dash of cayenne, and a bouquet of herbs. Cover the saucepan and boil for a quarter of an hour. Remove the herbs, add a piece of butter the size of an egg, a small cupful of cream at the last moment, and serve hot in the shells covered with the sauce. The cream is not indispensable, but improves the quality. When Homard à l'Américaine forms part of the menu, finger bowls are placed before each guest, and the serviettes are changed before the next course.

CHAPTER IV

RAGOÛTS (STEWS)

THE French begin all their stews by browning the meat in butter, adding water or stock afterwards. This method causes the brown gravy so much appreciated by English people travelling on the Continent. A white washy-looking gravy is unknown in France; the plainest of cooks browns the meat she prepares.

Ragoût de Veau à la Rameses.

Specially recommended.

Ingredients:
Two or more pounds of veal, cut into pieces.
Quarter pound of fat bacon.
Two large onions or four or five small ones.
A lump of butter the size of an egg.
A bay leaf, sprig of thyme, and parsley tied together.
Salt and pepper.
Half pint of sour thick cream.

Place the butter in a " cocotte," or saucepan with a cover that closes hermetically. Divide it into small pieces so that it melts equally. Cut the bacon into thin slices and place them on the top of the butter so as to cover the bottom of the pan; lay the slices one beside the other. Above this layer of bacon throw in the onions cut in rings, and the bunch of herbs. Put the pan on the fire and leave it uncovered. The veal is now salted and peppered on one side, turned, and salted and peppered again; and when the contents of the pan begin to smoke, add the meat. Cover it hermetically and stew on a slow fire for an hour and a half. Remove the pieces of veal and bacon with a ork; put them on a hot dish; throw away the bouquet of herbs; put the stew-pan on the fire again and add the sour

cream, stirring it constantly to detach the glutinous sub-
stances at the bottom of the pan.   Pour the sauce, which
is now a golden brown, through a colander over the meat,
and serve at once.   If the cream is too fresh, it can be
soured by pouring it into a good spoonful of vinegar and
mixing well.   Serve with a dish of dry rice, boiled in salted
water for twenty minutes.

Ragoût de Mouton (the French for Irish Stew).

Put the " cocotte," or stew-pan, on the fire to warm,
throw in a lump of butter the size of an egg.   When melted
and steaming, add the pieces of mutton, salt and pepper
them, and let them brown in the butter on both sides.
When a deep colour, remove them with a fork to a dish.
Peel a dozen or so of potatoes, cut them into halves or
quarters, according to the size—and in preference cook a
small waxy potato that will not require cutting; add a
turnip or two; throw them into the stew-pan; let them
brown in the same way as the mutton.   Add a couple of
large onions or half a dozen smaller ones cut into pieces;
replace the mutton; add a sufficient quantity of stock or
hot water, a bunch of the usual herbs (bay leaf, thyme,
and parsley).   Cover the saucepan and let the contents
simmer on a slow fire for two hours.   If the sauce is not
thick enough, remove a small quantity just before serving,
put it into a small bowl and add a teaspoonful of potato
flour (fécule) and pour it into the ragoût.   Skim the fat,
taste, and add salt and pepper if necessary.

Navarin (Mutton).

Melt some butter in the stew-pan, add a shoulder or neck
of mutton cut into pieces.   When browned, remove the
meat, and add a couple of tablespoonfuls of flour.   Turn
it quickly into the hot butter, and as soon as it becomes a
rich brown moisten with water; add salt, pepper, onions,
and a bunch of herbs (bay leaf, thyme, and parsley).
Replace the mutton in the stew-pan and let it boil on
a slow fire for two hours.   When nearly cooked, brown
some turnips in a little butter in the frying-pan and pour

them into the stew. Let them cook for half an hour, skim the fat, and serve. Potatoes and carrots can be used instead of turnips, or with them, according to taste.

Veau Marengo (Veal).

Cut a shoulder of veal into small pieces, throw them into a stew-pan with a lump of butter; let the pieces colour on both sides. Add chopped parsley and shalot, salt and pepper, a glass of white wine, and a couple of tomatoes. Stew for an hour and a half on a slow fire. Remove the pieces to a round dish, pass the sauce through a strainer, and pour it over the meat.

Bœuf à la Parisienne (Beef cooked in its own Gravy).

Take a piece of top-side of beef, put it into a saucepan with a lump of butter and a few onions; salt and pepper plentifully; turn the beef when browned on one side. When both sides are brown, cover the saucepan and let the meat cook on a slow fire for three hours and a half. Before serving, place the beef on the dish, add a tea-spoonful of potato flour (fécule) to the gravy in the saucepan, shake it a moment and pour on to the dish. No water is used in the preparation of this meat, which will be found excellent if cooked slowly.

Bœuf à la mode (Stewed Beef).

For this dish a piece of beef neither too fat nor too lean is required, not less than three or four pounds. If not sufficiently fat, it must be larded in the usual way, with narrow strips of fat bacon inserted into the meat. This operation is generally done by the butcher, but in many households the beef is not larded:

Ingredients:
A calf's foot.
A tumbler of water or stock.
A liqueur glass of brandy (not indispensable).
A bunch of carrots cut lengthways.
Two onions, a sprig of thyme, bay leaf, and parsley tied together, and a clove or two.

Place the beef in a stewing-pan with a lump of butter. Let it brown on both sides. Add a glass of water or stock and a small glass of brandy, salt and pepper; and the calf's foot, cleansed in cold water and a little vinegar (it should have soaked for an hour or more). After the contents of the saucepan have been brought to boiling-point the water is skimmed, and the carrots, onions, and herbs added; the saucepan is covered and the meat cooked on a slow fire, just simmering, for four and a half hours, and turned two or three times.

When the beef is tender when pricked with a fork, it is removed from the saucepan with the carrots, placed on a hot dish and kept warm while the fat is skimmed from the sauce. The calf's foot is not generally served with the beef; it is eaten on the following day with a piquante sauce. Salt, pepper, and a good spoonful of sugar are added, and the meat and carrots replaced, and served with the gravy poured over them. If not sufficiently thick, a teaspoonful of potato flour is stirred into the sauce before replacing the meat.

Bœuf à la Bourgeoise (*Stewed Beef with Olives and Tomatoes*).

Place a stew-pan on the fire with a lump of butter. When the butter steams add a piece of beef without bone, weighing between three and four pounds. Turn it on both sides until brown. Then salt and pepper well, cover the stew-pan and let it simmer for three or four hours, according to the weight of the meat. A quarter of an hour before serving stone half a pound of olives, and throw them in with the meat.

Cut four or five large tomatoes in half, horizontally; salt and pepper, and sprinkle the juicy part with a little chopped parsley and onion, and add a very small piece of butter. Put the tomatoes in a baking-dish into the oven for about twenty minutes.

Remove the meat from the saucepan; carve it in thin slices, and place one overlapping the other along the centre of a dish; pour the gravy over the meat, and garnish the sides with a small heap of olives and half a tomato alternately.

This meat is equally good the next day, if the weight be larger than is required for one meal.

Bœuf au jus (Beef).

Place a tender piece of top-side of beef in a " cocotte," or stew-pan, on the fire, with a lump of butter; salt and pepper the meat. Then cover the pan hermetically and let it simmer gently for three hours or more, according to the weight; when cooked, serve it on a hot dish, carve it in thin slices, and pour the gravy over it. No water or stock.

Épaule de Mouton Braisé à la Turque (Braised Shoulder of Mutton).

Select a lean shoulder of mutton weighing about four pounds. Remove the bone and roll it in the form of a long thick sausage, salting and peppering the meat in the inside. Tie it with thin string in several places. In Paris the butchers roll it and send it ready for cooking.

Place a stew-pan, or " cocotte," on the fire with a lump of butter. When it begins to brown, add the meat, turning on all sides to colour it. When the mutton is of a rich golden tint, throw in a dozen medium-sized onions—after having removed the outer skin. When these in their turn are brown, add the bones from the shoulder, salt and pepper again, and cover the stew-pan. Do not add any water. The mutton must simmer on a slow fire, with the pan hermetically closed, for two hours. Boil half a pound of rice in salted water for twenty minutes. Strain the rice, remove the bones from the stew-pan, and throw the rice in with the mutton. Mix it well with the natural gravy that has come from the meat; let it remain in the pan for a quarter of an hour, simmering gently with the mutton, and serve in a hot dish. The mutton is cut in slices (after the strings have been removed) or sent to table whole. The rice is placed around the meat, or in a mass, covering the centre of the dish, with the slices of mutton upon it.

Mutton à la Vinaigrette (*How to serve Cold Mutton*).

Cut thin slices from cold mutton, arrange them on an oblong dish, one slice overlapping the other. Make a sauce with two tablespoonfuls of oil to one of vinegar, a dessertspoonful of dry mustard, salt and pepper; mix well together and pour over the meat.

CHAPTER V

ENTRÉES AND PLAIN HOUSEHOLD DISHES

Poulet à la Crème (Chicken with a Cream Sauce).

Cut one or two chickens into two, rub them with salt and a dash of cayenne pepper.

Put a good lump of butter in small pieces into a stew-pan, and cover the bottom of the pan with thin slices of bacon. Cover the bacon with a layer of onions cut into rings, and put the pan upon the fire. When the contents begin to smoke, add the pieces of chicken, and let them stew upon a slow fire for an hour and a half. When ready they should be a light brown. Remove them from the pan, carve them and place them on a warm dish with the bacon. Put the stew-pan back again upon the fire. Add half a pint of sour thick cream, stirring constantly with a wooden spoon. Pour this sauce upon the chickens and serve hot. On no account add water to this sauce.

Poulet au Citron (Chicken with Lemon Sauce).

Boil a chicken with a handful of salt and three or four onions. The chicken can be carved after it is cooked, to serve as an entrée, or can remain whole if the carving is done on the table. In either case the sauce is thrown over it.

The sauce is made with the water in which the fowl has boiled, four eggs, and two lemons.

Break the eggs into a bowl, whites and yolks, beat them well with a fork or the egg-whisk; add a pinch of pepper and a couple of pinches of salt. Squeeze the juice from the lemons into another bowl, strain it, and mix it slowly with the eggs, stirring constantly. Then add gradually a little of the stock from the saucepan containing the fowl

—about three-quarters of a pint—and pour it into a jug placed in a saucepan full of boiling water, to thicken as for a custard. When the sauce is of the thickness of double cream, it is ready.

Remove the chicken from the saucepan, carve it, and place it on a hot dish; throw the sauce over it.

Curry from Singapore.

One fowl, one pound of rice, thirty grammes of curry powder, three tomatoes, two big onions.

Chop the onions and brown them in a saucepan for five minutes with salad oil and curry. Then add the tomatoes cut in small pieces, a little water, and let this simmer for a quarter of an hour. In a frying-pan place a piece of butter to heat, and throw in the fowl cut in pieces. When slightly brown, add the contents of the pan to that in the saucepan with two glasses of water. Let this simmer for half an hour. Salt and pepper. The rice is placed in a saucepan with enough water to cover the hand. Put on a quick fire until it boils, then let it simmer on a slow fire until cooked. The chicken with the sauce is served in the centre of the dish, surrounded with the rice.

Poulet au Blanc (Chicken).

Cut up the chicken and boil it in water with a handful of salt, a couple of onions, and a bouquet of herbs, for about three-quarters of an hour, or more if necessary, according to the age of the bird. Take a small saucepan, melt a piece of butter the size of an egg, rather more than less; add a good tablespoonful of flour; mix well with a wooden spoon and add a portion of the water from the saucepan the chicken has boiled in. Let this boil on a slow fire for about ten minutes. In the meantime break the yolks of three eggs into a bowl with the juice of two lemons, beat them well and add them to the sauce. The saucepan, after being taken off the fire, and the eggs intro-duced slowly, should be turned constantly to give the sauce a creamy appearance. Taste if sufficiently salted, add a pinch of pepper; remove the pieces of chicken from the saucepan, place them in a pyramid on a round dish, and pour the sauce over them. This sauce should be sufficiently thick to completely mask the chicken.

Poulet à la Génoise (Cold Chicken).

Boil a large fowl or capon with a handful of salt, keeping the cover of the saucepan hermetically closed. When the fowl is cooked, remove it into a colander and let it strain. Then place it in a deep dish, and pour the following sauce over it while it is still hot: A cupful of good salad oil, a cupful of vinegar, salt, pepper, a few pickled gherkins—finely chopped—a handful of capers, and, if convenient, a small glass of white wine. Let the sauce cover the fowl on all sides and remain in this " marinade " for at least twenty-four hours in a cool place. Turn the fowl from one side to the other. Serve it with a vegetable or green salad.

Ris de Veau Braisés (Braised Sweetbreads).

Given two sweetbreads weighing about a pound and a half to two pounds, the price of this entrée is not excessive. It is the very large " breads " that make the prudent housekeeper hesitate and fear lest the expense be too great. For a small entrée there is nothing to beat the sweetbread, but, like all food worth eating, it must be well prepared. And how few people understand the simple art of cooking sweetbread ! The first process is to put it into cold water, and change the water several times in order to cleanse it as much as possible. But no matter how long it has been lying in water, it must be bleached before the real preparation of cooking begins. To bleach it, put the sweetbread in a saucepan full of cold water, and let it slowly be brought to boiling-point. If it boils too quickly, the bleaching has not been thoroughly effected. As soon as the water boils, the sweetbreads are taken from the saucepan and passed in cold water. A stew-pan is placed on the fire, the bottom covered with a layer of bacon rind, to prevent the sweetbread from colouring. A carrot and an onion are cut into slices, a small bunch of herbs (a bay leaf, a sprig of parsley, and a sprig of thyme tied together) are added, and then, and only then, is the sweetbread introduced and covered carefully, first with a round of buttered paper the exact size of the saucepan, and then with the cover of the stew-pan. It is now placed on a very slow fire, and after five minutes or so a wineglassful of white wine is poured into it. And when this begins to dry and thicken, salt and pepper and a sufficient quantity of stock are added to nearly cover the sweetbread. The stew-pan is now put into a quick oven, covered, and allowed to cook for about three-quarters of an hour. The vegetables and bacon rind removed, the sweetbreads are placed on the dish; the sauce is passed through a fine strainer, and there is nothing more to do than to add salt and pepper, and the juice of a lemon, and pour it over the " breads " dressed and cut into slices in the centre of the dish.

Ris de Veau aux Pointes d'Asperges (Sweetbreads and Asparagus Points).

The sweetbreads are cooked in the same manner as in the preceding recipe, but only a portion of the sauce is poured upon them, sufficient to cover them but not to cover the dish. The asparagus points are calculated at half a small bunch for each person. They are lightly scraped and broken, in order to be perfectly sure that no portion of the edible branch is lost. When they are cut, it is impossible to tell exactly where the " wood " begins. The asparagus are then cut into small pieces, about a quarter of an inch long; the tips, in about a finger-length, are tied into a small bundle and thrown with the rest into a saucepan full of boiling water, not too much salted, and boiled for ten minutes without being covered, in order to retain their colour. They are then strained. In the meanwhile a piece of butter the size of a walnut is put into a small saucepan; as soon as the butter is melted, the saucepan is taken off the fire and a tablespoonful of flour added and amalgamated with a wooden spoon. Then the remainder of the sauce from the sweetbread is poured in; put on the fire again until just about to boil, with a pinch or two of pepper; and just before serving a certain quantity of butter is incorporated, always turned with a wooden spoon. The quantity of butter is calculated at about the size of a hazel nut per bunch of asparagus points. For six people, three bunches of " points " and three little lumps of butter. The asparagus is then turned into the sauce and served round the sweetbread, the little bunch of tips stuck in the centre.

Brains with a Cream Sauce.

Cook the brains in salted water. Make the usual white sauce with the water in which the brains have boiled. Add a cupful of cream. Place the brains in the centre of a round dish. Cover with the sauce. Garnish with slices of lemon.

Lamb's Fry.

Lamb's " fry " can be prepared in the same way as the sweetbread, braised with or without asparagus points.

Côtelettes d'Agneau Maintenon (Lamb Cutlets).

Half cook the cutlets in butter, one for each person. Make a thick béchamel sauce with butter, flour, and boiled milk (as explained in the chapter on Sauces); add grated cheese, about a quarter of a pound for six or eight cutlets, and a tablespoonful of onion purée, mixed with the cheese and the béchamel; salt and pepper. Place the cutlets on the dish that is to be served to table. Cover each cutlet with this thick compound, put it into the oven for a few minutes to colour. Pour the brown butter from the pan in which the cutlets have cooked over the dish that you take from the oven, and serve.

Côtelettes de Mouton à la Villeroy (Mutton Cutlets).

Take some small mutton or lamb cutlets, half grill them, and let them cool. Put a piece of butter and a table-spoonful of flour into a small saucepan, work one into the other and add a cup of milk. Mix it well with a wooden spoon until it thickens upon the fire. Remove the sauce-pan and add two yolks of eggs and half a cup of cream. Dip the cutlets into this sauce, which should be thick enough to entirely cover the meat, and let them cool on a tin. Then dip them in flour, then in egg, and then in grated bread-crumbs. Put a piece of butter into the frying-pan, and add a tablespoonful of good salad oil. When very hot fry the cutlets therein, and serve on a purée of potatoes, browned in the oven.

Escalopes de Veau à la Bourgeoise (Veal Cutlets).

Cut a number of small thin slices off a tender piece of veal. Break an egg into a soup plate, salt and pepper it and beat it well; in another plate mix an equal quantity of bread-crumbs and grated Gruyère cheese. Salt and pepper the slices of veal, and dip them into the egg and then into the bread-crumbs and cheese. Fry in butter and serve on a bed of dry rice, cooked in salted water for twenty minutes, covered with a tomato sauce. The small slices are well browned and arranged in a circle, one resting upon the other on the sauce.

Escalopes de Veau Nature (Veal Cutlets).

The slices of veal, in this instance, are cut much thicker, and should be about the size of the palm of a woman's hand, and as thick as an ordinary steak. Salt and pepper each piece of veal on both sides; put a lump of butter into the frying-pan, and when it steams place the veal in the pan. When the juice from the meat bubbles on the top, turn it; when the same occurs on the other side, the cutlets are sufficiently cooked. They are then served on a warm dish and the natural gravy in the frying-pan thrown over them. These cutlets can be served alone, or on a purée of spinach, or surrounding a pyramid of French beans.

Escalopes de Veau à la Parisienne (Veal Cutlets).

Small thin slices of veal are cut in the same way as à la Bourgeoise, salted and peppered on both sides, passed in egg and bread-crumbs, and fried in butter. Served with alternate slices of fried bread and rounds of lemon, dressed upon a circular dish, with a purée of endive in the centre.

Escalopes Visconti (Veal Cutlets).

Cut some veal into small slices, thinner than for the usual veal cutlets. Flatten them. Place them in a frying-pan with a piece of butter scarcely melted, taking care that the butter does not brown. Salt and pepper the small cutlets, turn them from one side to the other. Sprinkle them with chopped parsley, and when the meat is nearly cooked squeeze the juice of a lemon over them. They should be nearly white, not browned like the ordinary veal cutlets.

Caneton à la Rouennaise (Duck à la Rouennaise).

The real difference that exists in the qualification of a duck from Rouen or any other region lies in the manner of killing it. The Nantais, or Aylesbury, or Marseilles duck becomes a Rouennais merely from the fact that the blood is retained. The ordinary duck is bled. The Rouennais is strangled. There was an outcry some year or two ago against the Caneton à la Rouennaise, owing to the insufficiency of the cooking of the blood which made the sauce so widely esteemed. It has, however, since been discovered that ducks can still be prepared in this approved fashion if the blood is boiled. Consequently the Rouennais duck is now prepared in the kitchen, and not in sight of the guests as was once the custom.

Roast a duck twenty to five-and-twenty minutes. Remove the liver and chop it finely (the liver must not be roasted with the duck), salt and pepper it and throw it into a little hot butter and let it cook for two minutes. Carve the fillets from the duck and keep them warm on a hot dish. The pink gravy must be put into a special dish above a spirit lamp (or into a silver or china saucepan upon the fire). The carcase is pressed in an ordinary pressing machine, that costs about three shillings instead of the monumental press costing twelve pounds that the big restaurants thought it necessary to show their clients. Let the juice thus obtained be added to the gravy and allow it to boil; but when boiling-point is reached remove it and add the liver, a small glass of brandy, the juice of a lemon, salt and pepper, a little butter, and a teaspoonful of flour. Mix it all thoroughly, but do not let the sauce boil again. Pour it over the fillets of duck and serve.

Lièvre à la Royale (Hare).

This recipe for preparing a hare is famous for three reasons: the first because it was a favourite with King Edward VII.; the second because it is said to have been prepared by Senator Conteaux himself for his Royal guest; the third because it is of excellent flavour.

This dish comes from Poitou, a part of France that is as celebrated for its cooking as Rouen for pottery. A remarkable fact in connection with this preparation is that, although there is an abundance of garlic and shalot, the effect of one, so to speak, counteracts the other, and the guest never suspects that either of these powerful ingredients has been introduced into the hare.

Take a hare having passed the baby age. Kill it as cleanly as possible, in order to lose as little of the blood as possible.

Skin it, and remove the inside. Keep the blood and the liver.

Take about a quarter of a pound of fat bacon, a little

parsley, six cloves of garlic, eight cloves of shalot, a crust of bread soaked in water, and crumble it over the liver, the bacon, the garlic, and the shalot.   Break two eggs over this; salt and pepper and chop it all together as fine, as fine, as fine . . .

This preparation constitutes the " stuffing."   Fill the hare with it and sew the opening carefully together.

Line a stew-pan with rashers of bacon, and place the hare in it, in a circle.   In the centre put three onions, each onion stuck with a clove; a carrot cut into slices; salt and pepper.   Put the stew-pan into a hot oven. When the hare is browned, very brown, and the carrot and onions have given all the moisture they contain, pour in a glass of stock and let it boil for about five minutes, the necessary time to make the sauce.   The stock can be replaced by a glass of white wine.

The blood, which has been lying in a bowl, is now the chief ingredient of the sauce.   Pour into it three table-spoonfuls of flour, two tablespoonfuls of vinegar, two of brandy, mix well and work in, little by little, sufficient white wine to smooth it.   Pour this over the hare so that it partly covers it; add parsley, thyme, bay leaf, fifteen cloves of garlic, and thirty cloves of shalot chopped fine, and let it cook on a slow fire, simmering like a stew, for at least three hours and a half.

Put the hare on a dish, the sauce through a strainer over it.

The onions, carrots, and bacon must cook with the hare until the end.   The white wine can be replaced by red. The hare is served with a spoon.

Lièvre à la Darsy (Hare).

Cut a hare into small pieces, and remove the blood. Dry it with a cloth.   Put about a quarter of a pound of butter into a saucepan; add, when the butter steams, a glassful of chopped shalot, a tablespoonful of flour, and let them brown for about a quarter of an hour.   Then pour in a cup of cream, a cup of vinegar, and the juice of a lemon.   Into another saucepan put a piece of butter the size of an egg; throw in the hare, cut into pieces, but do not let it brown. Salt and pepper, and pass the sauce through a strainer over it. Add thyme, parsley, and bay leaf, and let it cook on a slow fire for two hours. Tie the herbs in a bouquet so that they can be removed before serving.

Champignons à la Crème (Mushrooms and Cream).

A dish of mushrooms prepared in the following manner is food for gods, and is served either as a vegetable after the roast joint, or as an entrée before it. For two pounds of button mushrooms put a quarter of a pound of butter and the juice of a lemon into a saucepan. Clean the mushrooms with a pointed knife and lay them on a plate, then throw them all together into a basin. Pour a little water over them and rub them for a minute or two, as mushrooms rubbed one against the other become white as milk. Throw them into a colander to drain, and thence into the butter and lemon in the saucepan. Put them on a quick fire, and let them boil for three minutes. Take another saucepan, a small one, put into it a lump of butter the size of a large egg, a tablespoonful of flour, salt, pepper, and a cupful of warm milk. Boil for ten minutes, stirring constantly with a wooden spoon. Place the mushrooms on a hot entrée dish, and throw the contents of the small saucepan over them.

Soufflé au Fromage (Cheese Soufflé).

For an ordinary sized soufflé dish for six or eight people, put a lump of butter—quite an eighth of a pound—into a small saucepan with two tablespoonfuls of flour. Mix one with the other with a wooden spoon on the edge of the fire; then salt and pepper, and add about half a pint of hot water, stirring constantly while it boils; add a quarter of a pound of grated Gruyère cheese, and a tablespoonful of Parmesan. Remove the saucepan and let it cool a little. Then break, one after the other, the yolks of four eggs therein. Beat the whites separately to a stiff froth in a bowl and mix them lightly with the contents of the saucepan, and pour into a buttered soufflé dish, leaving a couple of inches for the soufflé to rise. Cook it in a moderate oven for a quarter of an hour to twenty minutes, and serve immediately. If the top of the soufflé browns too quickly, cover it with buttered paper.

Poule au Riz (Fowl and Rice).

Put a quart of water, or stock, in a saucepan, with a piece of butter the size of an egg, a large onion cut into halves, a handful of salt, and pepper, a sprig of thyme, a bay leaf, and a little parsley tied together. When the water boils add a large fowl which has been prepared for boiling. In a couple of hours, or an hour and a half if the fowl is young, it will be cooked. About twenty minutes before it is finished remove the fowl into another saucepan, and strain over it the water in which it has been boiled. Wash a breakfast-cupful of rice and add it to the fowl. Cover the saucepan hermetically and boil slowly for twenty minutes. Place the bird on a dish, add a lump of butter to the rice, mix it well with a fork, and pour it over the fowl. If the rice is too thick moisten it with a little water. Taste to see if sufficiently salted.

Foie de Veau (Calves' Liver).

Cut the liver into slices, salt and pepper plentifully. Place a lump of butter in a frying-pan; add the liver when the butter has ceased spluttering. When the blood oozes turn the slices on the other side. Liver takes the same time to cook as steak, not longer or it becomes hard. Serve on a hot dish and pour the natural gravy around it.

Foie de Veau Roulé (Rolled Liver).

The liver is cut into slices of equal thickness, salted and peppered, each slice covered with the following mixture: a little chopped bacon, a little bread soaked in water, an egg, a little chopped parsley, and a small chopped onion, the whole worked into a paste. Each piece of liver is then rolled and tied with thin string or cotton, and placed in a frying-pan with a lump of butter. When the butter is hot, the liver is turned on all sides to brown, and a ripe tomato is passed through a sieve and added. The pan is then covered for a quarter of an hour on a slow fire; the strings are cut and withdrawn, and the rolled liver served with the sauce poured over it. This dish requires pepper in profusion.

Blanquette de Veau (Veal with White Sauce)

Cut a couple of pounds, or more, of veal, from the shoulder, breast, or neck, into cubic pieces of two or three inches. Put a quart of water into a saucepan with a handful of salt, a couple of onions cut in halves; a sprig of thyme, a bay leaf, and a little parsley tied together. When the water boils, add the meat, cover the saucepan, and let it cook for three-quarters of an hour on a quick fire. In a smaller saucepan place a lump of butter the size of an egg, and a little over a tablespoonful of flour. Mix the butter and flour together; add little by little— stirring constantly with a wooden spoon—the greater part of the water in which the veal is cooked. Let it boil slowly for about ten minutes; remove it from the fire and add the juice of a lemon, the yolk of an egg, and a good pinch of pepper. (The egg is not absolutely necessary.) Place the pieces of veal in the centre of a dish, and pour the sauce, which should be thick and creamy, over it.

A Veal Stew from the South.

For six people.

Two pounds of veal, two onions, three red chillies, four tomatoes, a little chopped parsley, salt and pepper.

Put a cupful of oil in a saucepan. When hot, add the veal cut in pieces and let them colour. Then a sprinkling of flour, a spoonful of tomato purée, a glass of sherry (or any white wine), water to cover, and let it cook an hour. Chop the onions, chillies, tomatoes, and parsley. Colour them, and add to the veal with salt and pepper, and let it simmer until quite cooked.

Rognons de Mouton (Kidneys).

Cut the kidneys into halves; grill them; salt and pepper plentifully. Place a piece of butter in a small saucepan; when it melts, add a tablespoonful of mustard and a little chopped parsley, and pour it over the kidneys on a hot dish.

Mouton en Chevreuil (Mutton).

Place the shoulder or leg of mutton in an earthenware dish. Throw over it a cupful of vinegar, a cupful of salad oil, two onions and carrots cut into rings, a sprig of thyme, a bay leaf, and parsley; pepper in profusion and a very little salt. Leave the mutton in this " marinade " for two or three days, basting and turning it occasionally. Remove the mutton from the " marinade " a quarter of an hour before it is to be cooked. Then place it in a baking-dish in a quick oven with a piece of butter. Salt it, strain the " marinade," and pour it into the gravy in the oven a few minutes before serving.

Filets Rossini.

Put a lump of butter into a low saucepan, and let it heat until it is brown. Cut thick slices from a fillet of beef, and cook them in this butter. Remove them when the blood oozes through the meat; salt and pepper. Place in the same saucepan in the same butter slices of foie gras, which must cook for about five minutes. Put a slice of foie gras on each fillet, on a warm dish. Moisten with a glass of sherry, a spoonful of tomato sauce, and some concentrated beef extract. Let this boil for five minutes on a quick fire. Just before serving add some foie gras about the size of an egg passed through a fine sieve, to the sauce, but do not let it boil. Pour the sauce over the fillets. The Filets Rossini are generally served upon rounds of fried bread of the exact size of the pieces of meat and foie gras, and the sauce is poured around them. It is customary to serve this entrée in a round dish.

Pain de Veau (a Family Dish).

Chop three-quarters of a pound of beef and three-quarters of veal as finely as possible; put two pounds of stale bread into a basinful of water; when soft, drain the water from the bread. Chop two small onions and a sprig of parsley. Break three eggs into a bowl, add the onions and parsley, the meat, the bread, and a teaspoonful of salt and pepper. Mix these ingredients with a wooden spoon until they are amalgamated. Shape the paste into a long mass (something like a roly-poly). Bake for an hour to an hour and a half, without water or fat. Serve cold.

Friture Mixte (Brains and Liver).

Brains and calf's liver are required for this homely and excellent dish. Break an egg in a deep dish, white and yolk together, with a pinch of salt. Beat it with a fork for a minute. Cut the brains into small pieces, about the size of a walnut, roll them in the egg, and then in the bread-crumbs. Cut the liver into pieces, round or square as they come, the size of the palm of a hand. Roll them in flour. Place a lump of butter in a frying-pan on a quick fire, and when steaming hot fry the brains and liver on both sides. When brown they are cooked. Serve on a hot dish, the brains and liver pell-mell in the centre, surrounded with slices of lemon.

Jambon à la Milord (Ham).

This is a dish to be recommended for a dinner-party, to be served before the sweet. It is very decorative and much appreciated by gourmets. For twelve to fifteen people the quantities are as follow: As many slices of cooked ham as there are guests, a mayonnaise sauce (see chapter on Sauces), a salad composed of half a pound of sliced potatoes, five artichoke fonds, a small bunch of asparagus points, and twelve walnuts.

Each vegetable is cooked and salted and peppered separately. Four or five leaves of gelatine, soaked in cold water, are added to the mayonnaise. The vegetables are mixed together, six of the nuts are broken and added, and the mayonnaise poured over them when the vegetables are cold.

The slices of ham are steeped in aspic jelly and placed upon the vegetable mayonnaise, one next the other, completely masking it. The top of the salad is flattened and decorated with slices of hard egg and the remainder of the nuts in halves (also steeped in aspic) forming a circle. The base of the dish is ornamented with chopped jelly.

Ham Pancakes.

Make the pancakes in the usual manner. Chop some ham as fine as possible, and let it colour in hot butter in a frying-pan. When slightly browned, add chopped mushrooms, a little tarragon, and some beef juice. Cook all together until it becomes consistent, without being too dry. Make the pancakes; and as each is removed from the pan, place a spoonful of the ham on it, and roll it up. Put the rolled pancakes in a dish in the oven, and serve hot.

Coq au Vin.

Take a fleshy chicken. Carve it in six or eight pieces. Place four ounces of bacon cut in cubes, a lump of fresh butter, and half a dozen small onions in an earthen saucepan, to colour. When a golden brown, add the chicken with parsley, thyme, and bay leaf, and a few mushrooms—if you like them. Cover the saucepan and cook on a quick fire until all is brown. Then remove the cover and skim off the fat. Pour over the chicken a small glass of old brandy and set light to it. Then add half a pint of good red wine, Burgundy in preference to Bordeaux, salt and pepper, and a thickening of butter and fine flour just before serving. When the chicken is cooked, place it on a hot round dish, pour the sauce over it, after removing the herbs, and serve surrounded with alternate slices of lemon and triangles of fried bread.

Stewed Giblets.

The giblets of goose or turkey make a succulent stew and is an excellent way of preparing the neck, liver, etc., of the bird.   The giblets are cut in small pieces and placed in a saucepan where a little lard has been heated.   About a dozen small onions are peeled and added, and, when browned, a tablespoonful of flour is sprinkled thereon, followed by a glass of water, half the contents of a small tin of tomato purée, salt and pepper.   This simmers for three-quarters of an hour, and then one pound of half-cooked chestnuts are added.   When the chestnuts are cooked, half a pound of grilled sausages are placed in the stew, the fat is removed from the gravy, and the contents of the saucepan placed on a warm dish and served with chopped parsley.

CHAPTER VI

IN France venison is not a food that is within the reach of small incomes, but in England, where it is plentiful, and consequently inexpensive, it may interest house-keepers to know how it is prepared by the ordinary French cook.

The Marinade for Venison.

Venison is never cooked in the natural state. After the skin and nerves have been removed it is larded and placed in a deep earthen dish with the following ingredients called a " marinade ": One tumblerful of vinegar, one of red or white wine, three carrots and one large onion cut in slices, three bay leaves and a sprig of thyme, salt and pepper, heated in a saucepan until on the point of boiling. The marinade is then put aside to cool, and when tepid is thrown over the venison. Once or twice a day the veni-son is basted and turned in the dish so that all parts are impregnated with the liquor. It is left in the marinade for three or four days.

Gigot de Chevreuil (Haunch of Venison).

After the joint has been skinned, larded, and placed in the marinade for four days, it is taken from the dish and cooked in a hot oven, in a baking-pan with several pieces of butter smeared over it, and basted with the liquor of the marinade, and is served with a sauce poivrade to which some of the marinade is added. (The recipe for this sauce is given below.)

Filet de Chevreuil (Fillet of Venison).

Is prepared in the same way as the cutlets.

Côtelettes de Chevreuil (Cutlets of Venison).

The cutlets are larded and put into a marinade for a few hours only. They are then placed in a saucepan, with a lump of good fresh butter and a sprinkling of pepper and salt, on a brisk fire, browned on both sides, and served with a purée of chestnuts into which the gravy from the cutlets has been incorporated. The chestnut purée is placed in the centre of a round dish, and the cutlets are lapped one over the other around it.

Sauce Poivrade for Venison.

Chop two onions of ordinary size, put them in a small saucepan with a little butter, and let them brown. Add a wineglassful of vinegar and the same quantity of red wine, a good pinch of pepper, five or six bay leaves, two sprigs of thyme, the same of parsley, two cloves, and a sprinkling of flour. Mix well together with a wooden spoon, and let the contents of the saucepan boil for three-quarters of an hour. Pass it through a fine sieve, and add the gravy from the venison. If the sauce is not thick enough, let it boil uncovered to " reduce " it.

When there is no sauce poivrade, a tablespoonful of flour is mixed with a lump of butter in a saucepan, the liquor of the marinade and the gravy from the cutlets are added and boiled for an hour. This sauce is then passed through a sieve into another saucepan. Fillets of mutton are often put into this sauce and eaten for venison.

Purée de Marrons (Chestnuts served with Venison).

Make a slight incision in the chestnuts before putting them in cold water, and let them boil until the outer skin can be easily removed with the point of a knife. Then put them on the fire in a saucepan with a little butter, and shake them until the second skin is loosened. Peel them and put them again in water with a little salt. When they are quite cooked, pass them through a sieve with some milk; add a little butter and the gravy from the venison with which you are serving the chestnuts, which must be as consistent as the usual vegetable purée.

CHAPTER VII

PASTIES AND PÂTÉS

CORNISH pasties, well known in England, have their equivalent in France under the name of " friands."

If it should happen, in a motor tour through France, you are passing a country inn on the stroke of twelve, it is worth stopping to luncheon on pasties, eggs, and vegetables, sometimes a " poule-au-pot," fresh fruit and cream, in preference to the heavy meat menus that the guide-book indicates at the restaurants on the road— menus made to suit the commercial travellers, staple clients who have not an idea in food above meat. The pasty as made in France, called " friand," is to all appearances a small sausage-roll, but make it as the French understand the pastry and the " friand " will take a place in a picnic or a country luncheon that the sausage-roll could never hope to hold, or even to aspire to. The very name of " friand " is in its favour, signifying " dainty."

Friands.

Let us follow the chef, step by step, as he prepares the pastry, and the meats that will line the inside of the paste for the " friands."

He pours a pound of flour into a bowl, with a pinch of salt; drops a quarter of a pound of lard and the same weight of butter into the flour, adds a little cold water, and mixes well with a wooden spoon. When the paste is in a ball, he turns it upon a board sprinkled with flour, rolls it once, a quarter of an inch thick, and cuts it in squares as for turnovers. He then takes an equal quantity of fresh veal and ham and chops it into small pieces, a pinch of pepper and salt, and adds sufficient sausage meat to hold the veal and ham together that he forms into sausages. Each sausage is placed into the centre of a

43

rolled piece of paste, the sides are flattened and tucked in, and the " friands " are put into a moderate oven on a baking-tin and baked until a golden brown. They can be eaten either hot or cold, hot if possible.

Pâtés.

Pâtés are generally made during the shooting season, and are found a valuable addition at a picnic or at the family table served with salad. They can be made with a crust or in a terrine. In a majority of households the latter is more popular, and when cold, slices are cut and served as required.

The " terrine " is an earthen vessel that can be placed in a hot oven without fear of breaking, and is to be had in many shapes—round, oval, or long—with a cover in the same ware.

Pâtés de volaille en Terrine.

> One pound of veal.
> One pound of young pork.
> One pound of fat bacon.
> One chicken.

Chop the veal, the pork, and the bacon as fine as possible. Mix therewith one egg, a good pinch of pepper, a little salt, and a pinch of the compound of laurel leaves, thyme, and cloves. (Dried in the oven, reduced to powder in a mortar with pepper, and passed through a fine sieve, bottled, and kept for use, the compound is made of equal quantities of herbs.)

Bone the chicken, season it, and place a little of the chopped meat inside. Now put a layer of the chopped meat into the terrine, and then place the chicken upon it; cover it with chopped meat, and on the top of all a layer of slices of fat bacon. Put the terrine into a moderate oven and let it cook for an hour and a half. Then remove the terrine and place a piece of wood or iron, the exact size of the terrine, upon the contents, and upon this piece of wood or iron a weight that makes all the fat rise to the surface. When cold, the next day, remove the slices of bacon and cover the pâté with melted lard to keep the air from it. Place the earthenware cover upon the terrine and cut slices from the pâté as required.

Pâté de Lapin (Rabbit).

One or two rabbits, boned; one pound of veal; and one pound of sausage meat make a good household dish. The veal and sausage meat must be chopped and placed beneath and above the rabbit in the terrine. When cooked (an hour and a half to two hours in a moderate oven), it must be weighted as in the preceding recipe, and on the following day covered with melted lard.

Partridges, pheasants, hare, ducks, and fowl generally, can be made into pâtés in the same manner, in terrines or in crusts, but the terrines are simpler for the ordinary household. A small glass of brandy or rum poured over the pâté is an improvement.

A Brittany Pâté.

One pound of veal, one pound of chicken cut in cubes, one pound of bacon, spices, salt, pepper. Chop finely, mix well into a smooth paste. Bake in a slow oven in a terrine, and when cooked cover hermetically with melted lard.

This pâté, like all the preceding ones, is eaten cold, and generally served with salad.

The making of this Brittany homely dish is very systematic. Every family, in certain districts, where the farm servants have to be catered for, prepare each week a pâté of this description for the Sunday midday meal. It is served afterwards, as long as it lasts, at supper, after the usual vegetable soup, and provides extra nutrition for men when required.

The pâté is, however, the food of only the richer among the Brittany peasants. The poor live on pancakes made of rye. Travellers may have noticed the fields of white flowers growing on red stalks under the cider apple trees, sometimes for many miles. These are the fields of rye for the national pancake.

Galantine de Volaille (*Turkey or Fowl Galantine*).

Galantines are made with any white-fleshed birds and are served in a coating of aspic. The ordinary ingredients are a boned turkey or fowl, a pound of fat bacon and a pound of sausage meat, half an ounce of pistachio nuts, pepper and salt, and a dash of cayenne. The bird, when boned, is flattened and covered with alternate layers of sausage meat and bacon, blanched nuts, plenty of seasoning and a truffle cut in slices. It is then rolled and tied in a cloth and placed in a long kettle of boiling water in which a couple of carrots, turnips, onions, and a bouquet of herbs, pepper and salt, have cooked for two or more hours.

The galantine must boil gently for three hours, and be pressed between boards, when removed from the kettle, until the following day.

Goose, " à la Française."

Cut a goose—or half a goose, according to requirements —into pieces. Place ten onions in a pan and brown with butter, add a little tomato purée and two pounds of boiled chestnuts. Salt and pepper.

CHAPTER VIII

ROASTS

On Roasts I have little to say. Nothing can equal the roasting of meat as known to the English cook. Meats of all descriptions are baked in France. Poultry is buttered before it is put into the oven and basted constantly; salted and peppered when the flesh is " seized." Chickens are invariably moister in France than in England —caused not solely by the quality of the birds.

In order to thicken the gravy of roast beef and veal, and to vary the flavour, French cooks pour about half a cupful of double cream into the pan a minute or two before removing the joint from the oven. The cream must be stirred into the gravy and remain in the pan just sufficient time to warm it.

Grouse, pheasants, partridges, snipe and game generally are delicious with the addition of a little cream that has been allowed to become sour, mixed with the gravy; or with fresh cream, made tart with a dash of lemon.

CHAPTER IX

SAUCES

Sauce Béchamel (White Sauce).

This is the simplest of sauces that every cook thinks she knows how to make, and that the majority of inexperienced cooks serve like a paste. In France the first lesson a novice learns is, that all sauces containing flour must simmer for ten minutes to a quarter of an hour after the flour has been mixed with the other ingredients. If this fact is remembered, there is no reason why an English white sauce should not be as good as the béchamel found so delightful in France.

Put a lump of butter the size of an egg into a small saucepan with two tablespoonfuls of flour; mix the butter and flour on the corner of the fire with a wooden spoon. Add half a pint of milk, and turn this mixture constantly with a spoon on a moderate fire for a quarter of an hour. When it is quite smooth and thick like cream, take it off the fire and add salt and pepper and another lump of butter, mixing well together.

This sauce is specially recommended served with hard eggs or vegetables boiled in water, such as cauliflowers and marrows.

Sauce Blanche (another White Sauce).

There is very little difference between the white sauce and the béchamel. A lump of butter is put into a saucepan on a slow fire and a large spoonful of flour worked into it until they are well mixed. Instead of milk, water is added, and the sauce is turned constantly with a wooden spoon for a quarter of an hour until quite smooth, and when ready it is salted and peppered and improved with an extra lump of butter as in the béchamel. If the sauce becomes uneven, a little cold water and a little more energy while stirring it with the spoon will remedy all defects.

Sauce Poulette.

Commence this sauce in the same way as the béchamel or white sauce. Add half a pint of hot water to the flour and butter; let it cook the necessary quarter of an hour; take it off the fire. Beat the yolk of an egg, add it to the sauce, with a little vinegar or the juice of a lemon, salt, and pepper.

Sauce à la Crème (Cream Sauce).

In the country this sauce is much appreciated, where cream is as easily obtainable as milk in town; it is excellent and quickly made. Put a bowl of cream into an earthenware or china saucepan, let it warm without boiling. Take it off the fire, add the yolks of two eggs, a small piece of butter, salt, and pepper, beating all together with a wooden spoon. For boiled fish, or to serve with asparagus, this sauce is unequalled.

Sauce à la Crème (a Sauce for White Entrées).

Put a little butter into a small saucepan, with parsley, chives, and shalots, chopped fine, a tablespoonful of flour, and a cupful of milk. Boil for a quarter of an hour. Pass the sauce through a colander into another saucepan, add a lump of good butter and a pinch of finely chopped parsley, salt, pepper. Mix with a wooden spoon.

Sauce Piquante.

Cut two onions into slices, a carrot, a sprig of thyme, a bay leaf, two cloves, two shalots, parsley, chives. Put them into a small saucepan with a little butter, place the saucepan on a moderate fire; when coloured a golden brown add a tablespoonful of flour, a little stock, and a

4

tablespoonful of vinegar. Boil it again on a moderate fire, pass it through a sieve, and season with salt and plenty of pepper.

Maître d'Hôtel (Butter Sauce).

Put a good lump of butter into a saucepan or earthenware pan, on a moderate fire. Chop a little parsley and chives, or parsley alone, and add to the butter, with salt and pepper and a dash of lemon. This sauce is poured over a steak or fish, or served in a sauce-boat, and is ready as soon as the butter is sufficiently warmed.

Sauce Hollandaise (Butter Sauce).

Melt a quarter of a pound of butter, more or less according to the quantity of sauce required. Throw in a handful of table salt and whip it with a fork until it becomes frothy. Pour it into a warm sauce tureen and serve with boiled fish.

Sauce Hollandaise (Another Butter Sauce).

A quarter of a pound of butter melted, the yolks of two eggs, a little lemon juice, pepper and salt to taste. Stir over fire till thick.

Sauce au Beurre Noir.

Place a frying-pan on the fire to warm. Throw into it a lump of butter; let it brown without burning. When hot, remove the pan from the fire and pour two tablespoonfuls of vinegar into the hot butter, salt and pepper, and a handful of capers.

Sauce Soubise (Onion Sauce).

Cut three or four large onions into small pieces. Put them into a saucepan with a lump of butter the size of an egg, on a moderate fire. When browned, add a tablespoonful of flour. Mix well together with a wooden spoon, add a cupful of hot water, salt, and pepper. Let it simmer for a quarter of an hour. Mix a little mustard with a tablespoonful of vinegar, pour into the sauce just before serving.

Sauce Remoulade (Cold).

Mix a tablespoonful of mustard with a tablespoonful of vinegar in a bowl; add four or five gherkins finely chopped. Break the yolks of two eggs into another bowl, chop a few leaves of tarragon and three shalots, and mix with the eggs. Add four spoonfuls of salad oil drop by drop, as if for a mayonnaise, turning briskly with a wooden spoon. Mix the gherkins in the first bowl with the sauce, and serve with hot or cold meats, or boiled fish.

Sauce Ravigote (Cold).

Boil two eggs hard, mix the yolks to a paste with four anchovies boned and scraped. Put them into a bowl with a spoonful of mustard, salt, and pepper; add four spoonfuls of olive oil, or good salad oil, turning briskly with a wooden spoon. Chop a handful of sweet herbs as finely as possible, and mix them with the other ingredients. The oil should be added very slowly, a small quantity at a time.

Sauce Tartare.

Place a small saucepan on the fire with a spoonful of flour and a lump of butter the size of a small egg; mix the flour with the butter and moisten with a glass of warm water; salt and pepper. Turn the sauce with a wooden spoon on a slow fire for a quarter of an hour, remove it when quite thick and let it cool. Chop three shalots, a sprig of parsley, a leaf or two of tarragon, mix them together. Beat the yolks of two eggs in a bowl with a spoonful of mustard, the same quantity of vinegar, the chopped herbs, and about four tablespoonfuls of good salad oil; add the contents of the saucepan with the cold white sauce, and the sauce tartare will be perfect if the eggs are fresh and the oil of good quality. So much depends on the quality of the oil in these cold sauces.

Sauce Mayonnaise.

Break the yolk of a fresh egg into a bowl, with salt and pepper, add drop by drop as much olive oil as the quantity of sauce required, beating the egg and oil together in the bowl with a fork or an egg whisk. Add a few drops of water, and a little vinegar when the mayonnaise is firm and creamy. The oil must be quite cold; the bottle is generally put under running water for a few minutes before starting the sauce.

Another Mayonnaise.

Mix a teaspoonful of flour with the yolk of a fresh egg in a bowl, with a tablespoonful of vinegar and a pinch of salt. Beat with a fork, adding drop by drop a little more than half a pint of oil.

Sauce Verte.

Boil a handful of spinach and squeeze the juice from the leaves through a fine cloth into a bowl. Add this green water to a mayonnaise sauce with some chopped tarragon, chives, parsley, and shalot. Served with cold boiled salmon or salmon trout.

Sauce au Kirsch (Kirsch Sauce).

Break the yolks of three eggs into a bowl with a little milk. Boil a pint of milk with a little sugar. Add the boiling milk to the eggs, turning them with a wooden spoon. Put the bowl into a saucepan full of boiling water, and let the sauce thicken on the fire. Remove the bowl and pour into it three tablespoonfuls of kirsch. This is a sauce served with sweet puddings or thrown over sponge cakes.

Béarnaise Sauce.

Break the yolks of three eggs into a bowl, with three spoonfuls of vinegar and a handful of tarragon chopped fine. Salt and pepper, and place the bowl in a saucepan of boiling water on the fire, and turn it with a wooden spoon when it begins to thicken. Add a little more tarragon if necessary, and pour into a warm sauce tureen.

Another Béarnaise.

Put three tablespoonfuls of vinegar into a small saucepan on a quick fire, with a handful of chopped tarragon, a few chives and shalots, all chopped as finely as possible. Remove the saucepan when the vinegar has nearly evaporated. Pour the contents of the saucepan into a bowl, break the yolks of three eggs therein, salt and pepper, and place the bowl in a saucepan of boiling water on the fire to thicken. Add some finely chopped tarragon at the last moment, mixing it with the sauce, which should be as thick as cream and as smooth.

Sauce Tomate (Tomato Sauce).

Cut four or five tomatoes into three or four pieces. Put them into a saucepan with two onions cut into slices, a sprig of thyme, a bay leaf, and a little parsley, salt, and pepper. Let them boil for a quarter of an hour, turning them occasionally to avoid burning. Pass them through a fine sieve and replace the purée in the saucepan, with a lump of butter and a small spoonful of flour. Let the sauce boil a few minutes and serve.

If tomato sauce is served in a sauce tureen, it is generally thickened with a sprinkling of flour; if it is required to cover a dish of macaroni, it does not need thickening with flour.

Bottled tomatoes or tomato sauce preserved in tins are treated in the same manner, as a good tomato sauce must be very much seasoned to satisfy epicures.

Sauce Cumberland.

Chop, as finely as possible, two shalots. Put them into a saucepan with the rind of an orange and of a lemon cut into small thin strips. Add a little water; boil for twenty minutes and strain off the water. The rinds and the shalots are then put into a bowl with six tablespoonfuls of red currant jelly, a pinch of ginger, a little cayenne, the juice of a lemon and of an orange. This sauce is served cold with cold game.

CHAPTER X

Lettuce Salad.

Cut lettuce leaves into pieces, not small, throw them into a basin of cold water with a handful of salt. Drain them in a wire salad basket, and shake the basket several times to remove any water that may still be on the leaves. Mix in a salad bowl the following dressing:

For an ordinary bowl of salad for three or four people (one cos lettuce, or two cabbage lettuces) pour salad oil, the best to be had, into a tablespoon with a couple of pinches of salt and pepper; stir over the salad; then add another spoonful of oil and one of vinegar, and mix well together with a spoon and fork. If the salad is in a larger quantity than specified, the dressing must be increased, but always to the extent of double the quantity of oil to vinegar. A teaspoonful of mustard can be added to vary the flavour.

Add, if convenient, half a dozen tarragon leaves cut into pieces. Wash them in cold water first.

Water-cress Salad.

Wash a bundle of water-cress, and cut into pieces, neither too small nor too large. Drain in a salad basket and shake the basket as in the preceding recipe, and mix with one tablespoonful of vinegar and two tablespoonfuls of best salad oil; salt and pepper.

Endive, chicory, escarol, are all treated in the same way.

Corn Salad and Beetroot.

Slices of beetroot are added to a corn salad and mixed in the same way.

White Endive.

The vegetable known as " endive " is often made into salad, as it comes at a time when there are few green salads. The crisp white leaves are cut into two or three pieces and mixed with oil and vinegar in the ordinary proportions.

Potato Salad.

Boil the potatoes in their skins, peel them when cooked, and cut them into slices—not too thick—add salt and pepper in equal quantities, and mix with oil and vinegar and a little chopped chervil.

Another Potato Salad.

Cut the potatoes, when boiled and peeled, into a salad bowl, with salt and pepper, and mix with a mayonnaise. Sprinkle with capers before serving.

Celery Salad.

Cut a head of celery into small pieces—throw them into cold water, strain in a salad basket; mix a tablespoonful of vinegar, two tablespoonfuls of oil, a teaspoonful of mustard, salt, and pepper, in a salad bowl. Add the celery and mix well. Beetroot can also be added to the salad if liked.

French Bean Salad.

Boil the quantity of French beans required. Cut them into halves if too large, and serve as a salad with the usual oil and vinegar dressing (one spoonful of vinegar to two of oil; salt and pepper). The beans must be cold before they are made into a salad.

Vegetable Salad.

Carrots, turnips, peas, beans, flageolets, potatoes, are boiled. When cold, the carrots, turnips, and potatoes are cut into small cubes, the peas and beans are added in the salad bowl, and a dressing is made of oil and vinegar in the quantities prescribed in the preceding recipes.

Russian Salad.

A vegetable salad made with a mayonnaise dressing (see Mayonnaise Sauce).

When fresh vegetables are not obtainable, a tin of " Macédoine " is bought, comprising cooked vegetables cut into cubes. The tin is opened and the vegetables are thrown into a strainer, and boiling water poured over them to remove any flavour of the tin. Carrots, turnips, and potatoes are added as in the vegetable salad proper, and " dressed " with the ordinary oil and vinegar dressing or a mayonnaise.

Tomato Salad.

Choose sound tomatoes, not too ripe. Wipe each fruit with a cloth to remove every particle of dust—but do not wash tomatoes. Cut the tomatoes into chunks, *not* slices, in a salad bowl; add one small onion chopped fine, one tablespoonful of vinegar to two tablespoonfuls of oil, plenty of salt and pepper.

Salade Malgache.

Cut up equal quantities of cold boiled potatoes, boiled celery root, and beetroot. Mix with mayonnaise, and add a thick coating of the sauce to completely mask the contents of the salad bowl. Build the salad in a pyramid and sprinkle with chopped peeled walnuts.

Salade d'Artichauts (Artichoke Salad).

Boil six artichokes, separate the " fonds " from the leaves, and cut them into small pieces. Place them in a salad bowl with an equal quantity of asparagus points that have been cooked in salted water. Take a handful of salted almonds, chop them fine; pound with them the juice of a couple of lemons and a cup of cream, pepper and salt, and pour over the salad. This salad can also be seasoned with a mayonnaise, but it loses somewhat of its delicacy.

Salade Ambassadeur.

Boil a couple of pounds of French beans with a handful of salt. If the beans are too long, break them in halves, but do not cut them. When tender, strain them and let them cool. Place them in a salad bowl with a little chopped parsley, and a pound of fresh tomatoes cut into chunks, and season with salt, pepper, and two spoonfuls of oil to one of vinegar.

New Salads.

Salads have become important items in the menu; and as almost any vegetable and a number of winter fruits are added, the dish is as nourishing as either meat or fish when the latter are eaten in small quantities.

A favourite salad is composed of lettuce, bananas, and apples, peeled and cut in slices, mixed with salt, pepper, oil, and vinegar.

Another is of raw celeriac, finely cut in strips the size of a lucifer match, with apples and walnuts covered with a mayonnaise sauce. The quantity of each must depend on the number of guests, and necessarily the apples are peeled and cut in pieces, and the walnuts taken from their shells and halved.

Celery salad is made with bananas, apples, chicory, and celery, all cut in small pieces and mixed with cooked ham, which gives a pinkish tint to the salad when the seasoning of oil, vinegar, salt, and pepper is added.

Japanese Salad.

Cook rice as for curry. For one pound of rice take half a pound of cooked peas, an onion cut in slices, two tablespoonfuls of salad oil, one of vinegar, salt and pepper, and mix all together as for an ordinary salad.

CHAPTER XI

VEGETABLES

THERE is a principle in cooking vegetables that must be established before entering into the minor details of seasoning, a principle which may make the old-fashioned cook shrug her venerable shoulders and lift her hands from her thighs. I am arriving at it slowly to prepare the imagination for an upheaval. Here it is. Vegetables must be boiled in as little water as possible. No steaming saucepans of boiling water to cover a handful of cauliflower, peas or beans, carrots or turnips, but water just sufficient to moisten, to be added to at times as required.

Doctors who have studied the important question of the preparation of food agree that the greater part of the nutrition in vegetables remains in the water wherein they boil. We eat, as it were, the husks when we have vegetables boiled in the customary way.

The same applies to dried vegetables, to peas, beans, and lentils. A very little cold water is necessary to start the cooking of either of these, and as they swell hot water is added in small quantities. Dried vegetables should be soaked for twelve hours if possible, and cooked slowly for three at least. As a digestive, nutritious food there is nothing better than a purée of beans or lentils. The weakest can digest purées.

To make vegetables palatable a handful of salt must be thrown into the water in which they cook. When they are tender, they are poured into a strainer to drain. A lump of butter is put into a frying-pan, and when melted the vegetable is thrown into the pan, tossed or turned with a wooden spoon, sprinkled with pepper, and a little chopped parsley (if liked), and served hot. French beans, carrots, turnips, celery, peas, white beans, lentils, cabbage, are all treated in the same way—*i.e.*, cooked in small quantities of water, and tossed in butter when drained; peppered and salted. If vegetables are fresh, they should be very palatable; if they do not taste deliciously, they have either not been sufficiently salted and peppered, or the butter has not been of good quality. Those who want to economise in butter and use an inferior quality called " cooking butter " should refrain from seasoning their vegetables with anything but salt and pepper.

Dried vegetables are placed in cold water; fresh vegetables in hot water.

Haricots Verts (French Beans).

Break the beans into two or three pieces, but do not *slit* them. French beans, scarlet runners, or any long green beans lose their properties if cut into shreds, as they are by most inexperienced cooks in England. If the beans are too long to serve intact, cut or break them across, in their width, not in their length. Throw them into cold water to wash them. Pour them into a strainer. Place a small quantity of hot water and a handful of salt into a saucepan—sufficient water to just cover the beans. When the water boils, throw in the beans and cook until tender, adding hot water when necessary.

Remove them by pouring the contents of the saucepan into the strainer. Melt a lump of butter in a frying-pan and pour in the beans. Turn them for a minute or two with a wooden spoon. Sprinkle with pepper and they are ready.

Haricots Verts à la Crème (French Beans and Cream).

The same as the preceding recipe, with a small cupful of double cream for a dishful of beans, added at the last moment and mixed with a spoon and fork, when the beans are ready for serving in the entrée dish.

Beans and cream are not served with meat, but as a vegetable alone.

How to cook Spinach.

The question of the cooking of spinach seems to be interesting the English public at the present moment, and I venture to think that a few recipes as prepared in French households may prove welcome to some of the uninitiated. First of all, I would like to dispel the belief, so prevalent in England, that butter, as used in the cooking of vegetables in France, renders them indigestible, or, as the current expression has it, " bilious." This is a mistake on the face of it, as biliousness—almost unknown in France—is a national illness in England, caused not only by the heavy consumption of meat, but by the insufficient time given to the preparing of many vegetables, notably cabbages, which form part of the Englishman's daily food. Butter is indispensable to the flavouring of vegetables, and is not in any way injurious to the health. To return to spinach. As a general rule it is estimated that for a dish of spinach—where it is not meant as an apology but a dish that is nutritious and intended to be partaken of freely—one pound is required per person. No matter what the dressing of the spinach may be, the starting-point is always the same. It must be well washed, changing the water several times, then thrown into a saucepan of boiling water with a handful of cooking-salt to boil for two or three minutes without covering the saucepan. The spinach is thereupon strained and placed under the tap of running cold water while it is in the colander, squeezed between the hands and either chopped very fine or passed through a wire sieve. For five or six pounds of spinach about a quarter of a pound of butter is placed in a stew-pan, and when steaming hot the spinach is added, and turned rapidly with a wooden spoon to dry it without giving it time to lose its colour. Salt and pepper are sprinkled in moderation, with a pinch of sugar, and the vegetable is served as hot as possible, surrounded with cubes of bread fried in butter.

Spinach à la Crème.

Prepare in as the preceding recipe with a teacupful of double cream added to the spinach before it is taken from the stew-pan to be served.

Spinach with Various Dressings.

Pluck the leaves from the stems of spinach. Wash the spinach carefully; shave it dry, throw it into a saucepan of boiling water for five minutes; remove it and throw it into cold water; press all the water out of it, hash it, pass it through a sieve; put it into a saucepan with two ounces of fresh butter, salt, and pepper; after five minutes it will be cooked. Have ready the yolk of a fresh egg with which you have incorporated two dessertspoonfuls of fresh thick cream; mix with the spinach. Now dish up the spinach with a garniture of fried crusts of bread, or with eggs poached in a poacher, or with hard-boiled eggs cut in half. Instead of the yolk of egg and cream, a good clear gravy or meat juice may be used; in this case garnish with fried ham, or braised ham, or tiny sausages, or with poached eggs. For six persons, four pounds of spinach if the leaves are young, three pounds if mature. Plenty of salt and pepper.

Epinards (Spinach).

Pluck and wash the spinach leaves. Throw them into a saucepan of boiling water and salt. When tender remove them, chop them on a board, pass them through a strainer, and throw them into melted butter in a frying-pan, with pepper.

Chou-fleur au Gratin (Cauliflower).

Cut the flowers with their stalks from a large cauliflower. (Select it " close " and not too full blown.) Throw them into a basin full of water with a little salt, to kill any insect that may be hidden. Put sufficient water into a saucepan, with a handful of salt, to cover the flowers. When the water boils, put the cauliflowers into it and cook until tender. Drain through a strainer and place each piece of flower, stalk upwards, into an ordinary pudding basin; fill the basin, always with the heads of flower downwards, until all the cauliflower is in it, the loose pieces at the last. Press them a little and turn them out on a dish. Throw a béchamel sauce over the cauliflower (that should now have its original shape), grate a little Gruyère or Parmesan cheese over it, and put into the oven for a few minutes.

The sauce is made with a lump of butter in a small saucepan, a tablespoonful and a half of flour, salt and pepper; mix one with the other and add half a pint of hot milk, turning the sauce for about ten minutes while it boils and becomes as thick as cream.

Chou-fleur à la Sauce Blanche (Cauliflower).

Is cooked in the same manner, the white sauce being thrown over it, if possible in a round dish, as it looks more appetising with the sauce surrounding the pyramid of cauliflower.

Cauliflowers can also be made into a salad when boiled as indicated and left to cool. The dressing of oil, vinegar, salt, and pepper (two spoonfuls of oil for one of vinegar), and a little chopped parsley is made in the salad bowl and the cauliflowers turned into it.

Petits Pois à la Française (Green Peas).

Shell the peas and put them into a saucepan with a lump of butter the size of an egg, and a glass of water for every two quarts of the shelled peas. Put the saucepan on the fire, mix with a wooden spoon, and add a small bouquet of parsley, salt, pepper, and another lump of butter. Peel a dozen small onions and add them to the peas. Let them cook for about an hour, covering the saucepan with a soup plate full of water. Remove the parsley and serve.

Petits Pois au Sucre (Green Peas).

Shell the peas and cook them as in the preceding recipe, with a little water and butter, onions, and salt. Add powdered white sugar to taste. It is essential to shake the saucepan occasionally, in order to prevent the peas attaching themselves to the bottom of the pan. It is as well to avoid using a spoon, as the peas are liable to be crushed.

Petits Pois au Lard (Green Peas).

Cook the peas in the manner indicated above à la Française. Cut into small pieces a few slices of bacon. Put them into a saucepan on the fire. When sufficiently cooked, add the peas.

Petits Pois à la Crème (Green Peas).

Boil the peas in water with a little salt. When tender strain off the water. Take another saucepan—earthenware if possible—throw in the peas with a lump of butter. Do not let the butter melt too quickly. It suffices to put the saucepan on the side of the fire to keep the peas warm. When the butter is well mixed with the peas, pour into the saucepan a cupful of cream; shake the saucepan and serve.

Petits Pois à la Parisienne (Green Peas).

Throw the shelled peas into a saucepan with a lump of butter and a little salt. Put the saucepan on the fire, and mix the peas and butter with a wooden spoon. Add ten or twelve small onions, a cabbage lettuce, or the heart of a cos lettuce. Let them cook for an hour without water, as the lettuce will moisten them sufficiently. Add another lump of butter and a little sugar, and serve with or without the onions.

Carottes à la Vichy (Carrots).

After having scraped the carrots, they must be cut into thin slices and put into a stew-pan with a lump of butter, a little salt, and a little sugar. Water is added, just sufficient to cover them, and they are then allowed to boil on a quick fire until there is no more water left in the pan, and the carrots are consequently dry and begin to brown in the butter. A pinch of chopped parsley is added, and the carrots are served as hot as possible.

Carrots as served in the Country.

A lump of butter is placed in a saucepan with two table-spoonfuls of flour, salt and pepper, and mixed with a wooden spoon. A pint of milk is boiled and added little by little to the flour and butter, and constantly turned with the spoon until the sauce is thick and creamy. The carrots are scraped and cut into round slices of medium thickness, and thrown into this sauce to simmer, with the saucepan covered, on a slow fire until cooked. A few branches of parsley are washed and drained in a cloth, chopped fine and sprinkled over the carrots before serving. This manner of preparing carrots has the advantage of retaining all the nutritive qualities and preventing the " watery " taste that many people object to in this vegetable.

Carrots with Béchamel Sauce.

Take a bunch of new carrots, scrape them with a sharp knife, cut them in halves, or in quarters if they are of abnormal size, and put them in a stew-pan with a lump of butter and sufficient water to cover them. Let them boil on a quick fire, adding a sprinkling of salt and a little sugar. The carrots should be almost dry when cooked, if allowed to boil with the saucepan uncovered. Make a béchamel sauce with butter, flour and boiled milk, salt and pepper; remove the carrots to a hot dish and pour the sauce over them.

Macédoine de Légumes (*Young Carrots, Turnips, Onions*).

Scrape a bundle of young carrots and a bundle of young turnips; peal a couple of dozen small onions. Place them in separate saucepans with a lump of butter and a teaspoonful of sugar. Let them brown for a few minutes, turning them with a wooden spoon; then cover them and let them finish cooking. Serve in alternate heaps around braised or roasted meat, or mix all together and serve as a vegetable stew, covering them with their natural gravy.

Artichauts à la Paysanne (*Globe Artichokes*).

Select large artichokes, place them in boiling water with a handful of salt, and let them cook for about half an hour. Then strain them. Put a small piece of butter, half the size of an egg, into a stew-pan, with ten or twelve small onions, two or three rashers of bacon cut into cubes, and a small spoonful of flour; turn the onions and bacon on all sides with a wooden spoon, and let them brown. In the meanwhile cut the artichokes in quarters if they are large, or in halves if small, remove the " beards," and tie each quarter or half with a thin piece of string or cotton. Take the onions and bacon from the pan, put the pieces of artichoke in their place, and let them colour slightly. Then replace the onions and bacon, add a teacupful of water, salt and pepper; cover the stew-pan, and cook on a slow fire for an hour and a half to two hours. Serve the artichokes in a hot dish, with the contents of the pan poured over them, as a vegetable alone. Remove the cotton or string.

Artichauts à la Vinaigrette (*Globe Artichokes, Cold*).

Boil the artichokes in hot water, letting them cook for an hour or more, according to size. When the leaves come from the artichokes easily, they are " done." Strain them, and let them cool. Make a sauce of oil and vinegar, salt

5

and pepper—the oil and vinegar in equal parts—and serve the artichokes whole, one for each person; the sauce in a sauce-boat.

Chicorée Frisée (Endive).

Endive, known as a salad in England, is excellent when cooked as a hot vegetable to be eaten alone or with meat. In families where economy is studied, the heart, or inner portion where the leaves are white, is washed and made into a salad with oil and vinegar, pepper and salt; the remainder washed, and cooked like spinach. The vegetable known as " endive " in France is short and white, something like sea-kale in appearance, but thicker and closer. Lettuces can be cooked in the same way.

Endive.

White, short, compact, and crisp leaves form the endive known as " endive " in France. They have something of the appearance of celery, but are smoother, fuller, and smaller. Wash a number of endives; remove the discoloured leaves, if any; throw them into boiling salted water, and let them boil for five minutes. Place them in an earthenware dish, after having strained them, side by side with sufficient melted butter to cover them and a sprinkling of grated Gruyère cheese, and let them colour in the oven.

Endives (Braised).

After having boiled them for five minutes strain and put them in a stew-pan with plenty of butter, salt and pepper. Turn them from side to side on a slow fire until well browned; remove them carefully to a hot dish and pour the contents of the pan over them. Braised endives are excellent either as a vegetable alone or with roast veal.

Endives au Gratin.

A dish of endives that pleases the most jaded palates is nutritious and not expensive. The endives are boiled in salted water, and then removed from the saucepan and placed in a Pyrex or an earthenware dish that can stand the heat of the oven. A layer of béchamel or white sauce lines the dish, covered with the endives, and the remainder of the sauce is poured upon them. Grated Parmesan or Gruyère is sprinkled thereon, and the dish is put into the oven to brown. With this preparation, the vegetable is served as it comes from the oven, on a second dish, china or silver.

Escarol.

This is plucked, washed and boiled like chicory, strained and pressed and thrown into a stew-pan with a lump of butter, salt and pepper, and a dash of nutmeg, and served when steaming.

Romaine Braisée (Braised Lettuce).

Wash a dozen lettuces. Cut off the roots. Tie each lettuce together and place them in a baking-pan with a little stock. Cover it and put it into a slow oven for a little over half an hour. Salt and pepper, and double the lettuces in halves on a hot dish. Place a lump of butter in the stock in which they have cooked, add the yolk of an egg or a little cream, and pour over the lettuces.

Aubergines.

Select them as nearly as possible of equal size, wipe them with a dry cloth, cut them in halves lengthways, place them, inside upwards, in an earthenware dish, sprinkle them with salt and pepper, moisten them with good salad oil, and then grill them, basting with the mixture of oil, salt, and pepper. Serve as hot as possible.

Aubergines (Fried).

Peel the aubergines and cut them in slices. Make a batter composed of flour, egg, water, a pinch of salt, and a little olive oil. Dip the slices of aubergine into the batter and fry them in a pan of boiling dripping or lard.

Salsify (*Scorconera*).

Scrape each salsify, cut pieces a finger in length, and throw them into a basin of cold water with a tablespoonful of vinegar. Strain them, put them into a saucepan of boiling water with a handful of salt and a tablespoonful of flour. The water must be boiling when the salsify are added. When cooked, strain them again, dip them into a light batter and fry them a golden brown. The dripping or lard in which they are fried must be boiling before the salsify are inserted.

Salsify with Cream Sauce.

Scrape the salsify and throw them immediately into cold water with a little vinegar. Put a tablespoonful of flour into a cup with a little cold water, and add it to a saucepanful of boiling water on the fire. Then add the salsify, cut in finger lengths, and boil until cooked. Strain them and serve with a béchamel or cream sauce.

Salsify au Gratin.

After the salsify have been scraped, thrown into cold water and vinegar to prevent them discolouring, and boiled, they are strained and placed in a white earthenware baking-dish, with an alternate layer of grated Gruyère and cream or béchamel sauce, and finally, with a sprinkling of grated bread-crumbs, put in a hot oven for five or six minutes and served in the same dish.

Asparagus Points.

Break the thin green asparagus where it hardens, boil the points in salted water, and then throw them into a colander in cold water in order to prevent them from discolouring. Put a lump of butter into a stew-pan, add the asparagus points, with a little salt and pepper, and a pinch of sugar. Asparagus points are mixed with an omelette or with scrambled eggs.

Asparagus Points : a Hors d'Œuvre.

Cook the asparagus points in salted water, place them in a *hors d'œuvre* dish with an equal quantity of peeled shrimps and half the quantity of boiled sliced potatoes (previously boiled in their skins and sliced when cold). Cover with a mayonnaise and mix well together.

Stuffed Tomatoes " à la Provençale."

Select large tomatoes, very red and somewhat flat. Cut them in halves. Squeeze each half to eliminate the juice and the pips. Then put them in a dish and fill them with the soft part of a peeled tomato and bread-crumbs in equal quantities, chopped parsley, a small onion, salt and pepper. When amalgamated, fill the tomatoes with the stuffing, and cover with bread-crumbs and a little olive oil. Pour some oil in a pan without covering it, place the tomatoes in it on the stove, and, only when they begin to colour, put them in the oven to finish cooking.

Tomatoes " à la Couloumé."

Here the tomatoes must be very ripe and uniform in size, if possible. At the stalk, remove about an inch in depth, making a circle. Then mix peeled shrimps, hard-boiled eggs chopped small, and the heart of a lettuce, covered with a mayonnaise. Fill the tomatoes with this mixture; and on the top of each place a slice of pickled gherkin.

In order to improve the appearance of the dish, arrange the tomatoes on leaves of the chestnut-tree or vine.

This effect of red upon green is excellent.

VEGETABLES THAT FEW KNOW HOW TO PREPARE

Jerusalem Artichokes in Croquettes.

One pound of Jerusalem artichokes, one egg, half a glass of milk, two spoonfuls of flour, salt and pepper.

Boil the artichokes in salted water, peel them and pass

them through a sieve. Mix the flour with the milk, add the egg, and then mix with the artichokes. Throw this preparation, spoonful after spoonful, into hot dripping, and serve the croquettes thus obtained as warm as possible.

Jerusalem Artichokes with a White Sauce.

Two pounds of artichokes, salt, and a pint of milk, a little butter, flour, and a pinch of spice.

Peel the artichokes, and cut them in slices. Throw them into boiling water with a little salt. They are cooked in eight or ten minutes.

Make a white sauce with the flour, milk, and butter. Strain the artichokes, put them in the sauce, and let them simmer for a minute or two, and serve.

Jerusalem Artichokes " au Gratin."

Three pounds of artichokes, half a pint of milk, half a pint of water, butter (the size of an egg), and the same quantity of flour, a little grated cheese, salt and pepper.

Wash the artichokes when peeled, and cut them in thick pieces. Place them in an earthen or china saucepan, cover with water, add salt, and let them boil for two hours. (A tin or iron saucepan would make them black.)

Put the butter in a saucepan with the flour, and mix well. Then add, little by little, the milk and water (a pint), and boil for a quarter of an hour.

Strain the artichokes when they are cooked (the water can be added to any soup), cut them in small pieces and place them in a dish that will stand the oven, cover with the same, sprinkle with grated cheese, and serve when a golden brown. (For this preparation a Pyrex dish is excellent.)

MIXED VEGETABLES

Carrots and Potatoes with Bacon.

One pound of carrots, a quarter of a pound of bacon, two pounds of potatoes, thyme, parsley, and a bay leaf, salt and pepper, an onion and a clove, a little butter.

Cut the carrots in cubes after having well washed them; peel the potatoes and cut them like the carrots; cut the bacon in the same way; peel the onion and stick the clove into it; wash the herbs and tie them together.

Throw the bacon into the butter or margarine when heated in the pan; when cooked without being hard, add the carrots, stir all together, add the herbs, the onion, salt and pepper, and sufficient water to cover them, and let them simmer for an hour and a half. Then add the potatoes and cook again for forty minutes and serve.

(Turnips and potatoes, cabbage and potatoes can be treated in the same manner).

Pommes de Terre Soufflées.

There is no equivalent in the English language for pommes de terre soufflées, because there is nothing similar in English cookery. Potatoes are fried by English or foreign cooks in private kitchens, but they never reach the perfect state known as soufflées. In restaurants and some of the big hotels where cooking is an art, I should say a fine art, the chef will serve a dish of these golden little bags, piled symmetrically one on top of the other in pyramid form, each a perfect specimen of a pomme de terre soufflée, and the guests will acknowledge that the chef is an artist, and that nothing can compare with these potatoes from a gastronomico-artistic point of view—if I may be allowed the expression. And in London as in Paris, where these potatoes are served as a supper dish by themselves, or as an accompaniment to grilled meats, they are looked upon as curiosities, and everybody has a theory of his own as to how they are prepared. The general theory that the potatoes are submerged in two pans of hot fat is correct in a way, but the practice never shows the correct result. Cookery books by the score will give the recipe for pommes soufflées, but I have never known one single attempt that has proved the exactness of the methods indicated. If, however, the present instructions be followed in the minutest details, there will be no difficulty in conjuring a dish of potatoes fit for a king, each piece of potato being as perfect as those served by the most experienced and dearly paid chef.

The quality of the potato must be what is known as " Hollande " in France—and I suppose means a Dutch waxy potato in English. The potatoes must be selected sound. A deep frying-pan half full of fat, a wire skimmer and a metal strainer, a cloth and a plate are the " tools."

Put the pan of fat on the fire—the best fat for the purpose is melted suet. Peel five or six large potatoes; trim the edges, and with a sharp knife cut them *lengthways* into slices of equal width, of the thickness of two English florins, neither wider nor narrower, for in the cutting of the potato lies the success of the undertaking. (Amateurs would do well to practise cutting before frying.)

1st. Each slice of potato is then *wiped* with a cloth, and *not washed*, and thrown into the pan when the fat begins to heat. It is essential that at this stage the fat be not too warm. A dozen slices may be cooked at a time, not more. When sufficiently poached the slices will rise to the surface and have the appearance of soufflées— they will blister a little. They may then be removed with the skimmer, one by one, and kept warm at the edge of the oven.

2nd. The pan of fat is now heated to a greater degree, and when smoking and boiling, the poached slices are thrown in and quickly turned with the skimmer, and in a second the " drying " process is effected and each slice becomes a perfect soufflé, and is removed into the strainer and sprinkled with salt, arranged symmetrically on a hot dish, and served. These soufflé potatoes will keep their shape for hours—twenty-four sometimes—if successfully prepared.

N.B.—An unevenly cut slice will not " swell." A too thinly cut slice will brown. The potato must be cut with the grain. The science, therefore, of pommes de terre soufflées lies in the cutting.

Pommes de Terre Frites (*Fried Potatoes*).

Peel the potatoes and cut them into sticks the size of a finger of a normal woman's hand (the potato should not be very long), wipe them in a cloth. Place a pan half full of fat upon the fire. When the fat boils and steams, throw in the potatoes, turning them immediately with the skimmer. When they are of a light golden brown, remove them with the skimmer into a strainer, shake the strainer over a bowl to drain the fat, sprinkle with salt, and shake again that the salt may touch all the potatoes, and serve with or without a few branches of fried parsley.

Pommes de Terre à la Maître d'Hôtel.

Boil the potatoes in their skins. Peel them and cut them into slices, rather less than a quarter of an inch thick. Melt a lump of butter in a small saucepan, add a little chopped parsley, salt, and pepper, and pour the sauce over the potatoes.

Pommes de Terre Sautées (Potatoes).

Wash the quantity of potatoes required and boil them in their skins. Place a lump of butter in a frying-pan. When melted, cut the potatoes in round slices into the pan; turn them constantly with the skimmer; when slightly brown, sprinkle them with salt and chopped parsley, and serve hot. Good dripping can be used instead of butter.

Omelette aux Pommes de Terre (Potato Omelet).

Break the eggs into a bowl, two for each person. Beat them well with a fork; add salt and pepper. Melt a large lump of butter in a frying-pan. Throw in some rounds of boiled potatoes to colour slightly as in the preceding recipe, and pour in the eggs. When they are set, double the omelette in two as explained in the chapter on Omelettes.

Pommes de Terre Béchamel (Potatoes with Béchamel Sauce).

Boil the potatoes in their skins. Peel them and cut them into rounds as for pommes de terre sautées. Place them in a dish to keep warm. Put a lump of butter into a small saucepan, add a tablespoonful of flour, work one into the other, and pour in gradually half a pint of boiled milk, stirring constantly on the fire. Salt and pepper this

sauce, and let it boil gently for ten minutes; it should be of
the thickness of cream. Pour it over the potatoes and
serve with a sprinkling of chopped parsley and chervil.
This quantity of sauce is for a small dish of potatoes, and
can be served with or without the herbs.

Pommes de Terre au Lard (*Potatoes and Bacon*).

Cut some bacon into cubes or small pieces, fry them in
a little butter, add a tablespoonful of flour, a little stock or
water, a tumbler of ordinary red wine, a sprig of thyme,
a bay leaf, one or two onions, and pepper. When they
begin to boil, add potatoes that have been peeled and
washed, and cut into quarters or eighths, according to
size. Cover the stew-pan and cook for about forty
minutes. Remove the herbs before serving.

Equally good if made without onions or herbs.

Croquettes of Potatoes.

Boil the potatoes in their skins. Peel them when
sufficiently cooked. Drain them, and mash them with a
lump of butter; add three eggs, salt, and pepper; stir well
with a wooden spoon. Roll them into croquettes, long
or round. Break an egg into a soup plate, with a pinch of
salt; into another plate pour some grated bread-crumbs.
Roll the croquettes first in the egg and then in the bread-
crumbs, and fry a golden brown.

Potato " Friands."

Boil some potatoes in their skins in salted water.
Peel them when they have cooled. Make a paste with the
potato and some flour, sufficiently thick to be able to roll
it. Then cut it into shapes, round or square (according to
fancy), and cook these pieces in hot butter. When a
golden colour, sprinkle with sugar; or serve two at a time,
inserted with jam.

CHAPTER XIII

OMELETTES AND EGGS GENERALLY

How to make an Omelette

I employ the French word advisedly, because the English omelet has no relation to the French. The plainest of French cooks makes an omelette, I may say, intuitively. She has a light hand, and it is her nature to beat lightly, to work quickly, and an omelette must be made quickly. Some people imagine that the number of eggs is limited, and that more than twelve should never be beaten together. To a certain extent this is correct, but only to a certain extent—the extent of the pan. An omelette of more than twelve eggs cannot be made in a pan of the ordinary dimensions. In fact, there is no limit to the size of an omelette if the pan is of equal capacity. In the restaurants the omelette pans are rigorously kept for the purpose of this particular dish, and are merely wiped after they have been used, never washed. The eggs have not soiled it, and the cook considers it essential that the pan should remain " fat " (*gras*). But in the ordinary household where the same pan is used to cook a steak or fry potatoes, it is indispensable to wash it. A word more and we will begin operations. The pan should be thick, and the handle short; and a fierce fire cooks an omelette better than a dull one.

For an omelette of six or eight eggs, break them into a bowl, add salt and pepper, and beat them with a fork for about a minute, not longer as a rule. When the eggs are sufficiently beaten, they " run " off the fork in a homogeneous liquid, without any glutinous appearance. It is not necessary to beat for several minutes, with the idea that the more the eggs are beaten the lighter the omelette. This is a great mistake, as too much beating causes eggs to lose their consistency. It is, however, better to beat too much than too little.

Place the pan on the fire to warm it, put in a small piece of butter—about the size of an egg for an omelette of six or eight. Add the contents of the bowl when the butter steams. If this precaution is taken, the omelette will not catch, as the high temperature of the butter isolates the eggs. It is therefore a mistake to shake the eggs directly they are poured into the pan. But a second or two later the fork must be passed round the sides of the pan to loosen the eggs, and then they are worked in all directions with the back of the fork as if they were scrambled. When they are sufficiently cooked they look in fact almost like scrambled eggs; but now the omelette is shaken on to one side of the pan, and with the fork one half is folded on the other and slid on to the dish. The shape of the omelette is thus obtained without difficulty, and the heat of one half just finishes the cooking of the other as it rests upon it.

Omelette Soufflée (Sweet).

Take two bowls. Put into one of them three table-spoonfuls of white sugar; into the other a pinch of salt. Break five eggs, separate the yolks, and drop one yolk at a time into the bowl containing the sugar; whip them well with a wooden spoon and they become creamy like a mayonnaise. Add a little powdered vanilla to another tablespoonful of sugar, and mix with the yolks. Put the whites of the eggs into the bowl containing the salt and whip into a stiff froth. Mix with the yolks as lightly as possible, and pour the contents into a buttered dish in the shape of a pyramid. Cover it with sifted white sugar and leave it for three or four minutes on the side of the stove. Then put it into the oven for ten to twelve minutes, turning the dish occasionally to colour it on all sides. Make two or three incisions with a knife and serve imme-diately. This omelette must be eaten as soon as it is cooked, or it loses both its shape and its delicacy.

Another Omelette Soufflée.

There are several variations on the theme of omelettes. One of the most popular is to add five macaroons, pounded to powder, to the yolks of the eggs when they have been well amalgamated with the sugar. The same care must be taken in adding the stiffly beaten whites as in the preceding, and the omelette is poured into a buttered mould. A cake mould serves the purpose excellently. Let it bake in a quick oven for about twenty minutes. A serviette is pinned around the mould, as the omelette cannot be turned out. These omelettes can also be made in a soufflé dish. It is, however, difficult to say how long an omelette takes to bake, as everything depends on the heat of the oven. In order to ensure success, the best way is to look in and note that when it is sufficiently "raised" it is ready for table. In the preceding recipe the time calculated for the cooking of the omelette is shorter, because it comes into direct contact with the heat of the oven.

Omelette au Lard (Bacon Omelet).

Cut two or three rashers of bacon into small pieces, put them into a frying-pan with a small piece of butter. Let them colour on both sides. In the meanwhile break six eggs into a bowl, salt and pepper plentifully, beat them with a fork until well mixed, and pour them into the frying-pan that contains the bacon. Make the omelette in the ordinary way, passing the knife round the edge of the pan to prevent the eggs from sticking, add a little butter if the pan is not sufficiently "fat"; shake one half of the omelette on to the other when the eggs begin to "set," and serve on a hot dish.

Omelette au Fromage (Cheese Omelet).

Beat the number of eggs required for an omelette (generally two for each person) with salt and pepper in a bowl; add two or three spoonfuls of grated Gruyère cheese; mix well and pour into the pan, following the indications in the preceding recipes. If there is not sufficient butter in the pan, while the omelette is cooking a little may be added by slightly lifting the edge with a knife and dropping it beneath.

Omelette aux Fines Herbes (Herb Omelet).

A sprinkling of chopped parsley and chervil, or parsley, chervil, and chives, beaten with the eggs before they are placed in the pan, make an " omelette aux fines herbes."

Omelette aux Tomates (Omelet with Tomatoes).

Break the eggs into a bowl with salt and pepper; beat them for a few minutes with a fork, place the omelette pan on the fire to warm, add a lump of butter. When the butter steams, pour in the eggs. Make little incisions with a fork to let the heat reach the eggs in all parts; pass a knife round the edge of the pan to prevent the eggs from " sticking "; fold one half on the other as soon as they begin to get firm, and shake the omelette on to a hot dish. Pour over it a good tomato sauce made according to the simple recipe in the chapter on Sauces.

Omelette à l'Italienne (Italian Omelet).

This omelette is generally made with the remainder of a dish of macaroni, and will be found an excellent manner of utilising that which in some households is thrown away. " What can I do with cold macaroni ?" says the inexperienced cook. Read and you will know. The macaroni, which has been flavoured with butter, cheese, and sometimes with tomatoes, is cut into small pieces and thrown into the omelette pan in the steaming butter, after the eggs have been poured in. The same process of folding follows, and a nutritious, appetising omelette is the result.

Œufs au Gratin (Eggs with Cheese).

Toast as many pieces of bread as there are guests. Butter the toast and break an egg on each piece, leaving the yoke intact. Place these in a buttered dish in the oven, with a thin coating of Parmesan or Gruyère cheese on each. Serve hot.

Œufs à la Crème (Eggs).

Boil a dozen eggs hard (about seven minutes is the time allowed when the water boils). Remove them from the boiling water, and steep them in cold water to facilitate the shelling. Break the shells and cut the eggs into halves. Place them points upward on an entrée dish. While the eggs have been boiling put a lump of butter, the size of the largest egg, into a small saucepan, with two tablespoonfuls of flour, a good pinch of salt, and pepper. Mix well together with a wooden spoon, warm a pint of milk in another saucepan and pour it into the butter and flour, turning constantly with the spoon for a quarter of an hour on a moderate fire. Taste the sauce (which should be white, and as thick as cream), and add salt if necessary, as it must be remembered that the eggs have not been cooked with salt. Pour the sauce over the eggs and serve.

Œufs au Fromage (Eggs).

Put a quarter of a pound of grated Gruyère cheese into a small saucepan with a piece of butter half the size of an egg, chop parsley and chives, put in a little nutmeg and half a glass of milk or ordinary white wine. Boil on a moderate fire, turning the contents of the saucepan with a wooden spoon until the cheese is melted. Break six eggs into a bowl, salt and pepper and throw them into the melted cheese, and cook them like scrambled eggs, on a slow fire. Serve in the centre of a dish surrounded with toasted or fried pieces of bread, diamond-shaped.

Œufs au Pain (Eggs).

Put half a handful of crumbled bread into a saucepan with a teacupful of cream, salt, pepper, and nutmeg. When the bread is swollen with the cream, break six or eight eggs, beat them, and make an omelette.

Œufs à l'Aurore (Eggs).

Boil a dozen eggs—for six people. When they are hard, throw them into cold water, in order to remove the shells easily. Divide the white from the yolk and chop each separately. Put a lump of butter and a tablespoon-ful of flour into a small saucepan, stir the flour into the butter, add a glass of milk, and mix constantly on the fire. When smooth and creamy, add a piece of fresh butter, salt and pepper. Put a layer of this sauce into a deep dish, cover it with a layer of yolks and a layer of whites, another layer of salt, and so on; the yolks must be uppermost; then put the dish into the oven to colour.

Œufs mollets Béchamel (Eggs).

Boil a given quantity of eggs for a little under five minutes, the time to set them firmly without hardening. Steep them in cold water to facilitate the removing of the shells; place the eggs whole in a dish, and pour a béchamel sauce over them. Serve hot. (See chapter on Sauces.)

Œufs Bretons (Eggs).

Make a good tomato sauce. (See chapter on Sauces.) Pour it into the centre of a round dish, and keep it warm on the edge of the stove or over the smallest of gas flames. Place as much dripping in a pan, on the fire, as will nearly fill the pan when the fat is melted. Break the quantity of eggs required, one or two for each person, into a cup, one at a time, and throw each egg into the fat when it steams. With the skimmer cover the yolk with the white, and when the egg begins to brown turn it carefully on the other side for a second or two. Remove it with the

6

skimmer, letting the fat drain through the holes over the pan; place each egg around the tomato sauce, and sprinkle with a little salt and pepper before serving. This is an excellent luncheon dish.

Œufs aux Tomates (*Eggs*).

Poach the eggs and pour over them a tomato sauce. Or pour the tomato sauce into the dish that serves to cook eggs, put this dish upon the fire and break the eggs into it. (See chapter on Sauces for Tomato Sauce.)

Œufs aux Artichauts (*Eggs and Artichokes*).

Place a large saucepan full of hot water on the fire; let it boil; throw into it a handful of salt. Boil as many artichokes as there are guests. When the leaves come away easily, the artichokes are cooked. Remove the leaves and the " beard " and put the " fonds," one next the other, into a buttered dish. Break an egg into each " fond," add salt and pepper, and cook them in the oven.

Œufs au Beurre Noir (*Eggs*).

Put a frying-pan on the fire to heat; throw in a lump of butter; break the eggs therein when the butter has melted. Remove the eggs to a hot dish (a flat, round one is the most appetising for these eggs), add a little more butter, if necessary, in the frying-pan; let it colour without burning; take it off the fire, add a spoonful or two of vinegar, and a few capers. Salt and pepper and pour over the eggs.

Œufs sur le Plat (*Eggs*).

Melt a lump of butter in an egg dish; break the eggs upon the butter, salt and pepper, and serve as soon as the white has " set." The eggs must be perfectly fresh or the yolks will not remain intact. Serve immediately or the eggs become hard and leathery. If an egg dish is not to hand, a frying-pan can be used; but it is advisable to procure a dish of this description from any earthenware depot, as the eggs look prettier in their white dish, and are served hotter when not removed from the dish in which they were cooked.

Œuf Frits (Eggs).

Put a bowlful of dripping into a frying-pan. Put it on the fire to warm. When "smoking hot," break the eggs therein, salt and pepper, and in a few seconds turn the eggs with the straining spoon. Let the oil filter through, and serve on a hot dish, in a pyramid, with a sprinkling of fried parsley.

Œufs Farcis (Cold Eggs).

Boil some eggs hard; let them cool; peel them; cut them lengthways; remove the yolks carefully and mash them with a little salad oil, salt, pepper, chopped parsley, and chives. Fill the halves of the whites of each egg with this mixture; place them in a dish, one next the other; make a little salad dressing with two spoonfuls of oil and one of vinegar; add the remainder of the yolks that has not filled the whites, and pour the dressing over the dish of eggs.

Œufs Farcis (Hot Eggs).

Boil the eggs hard; peel them and cut them lengthways in halves; remove the yolks and mash them with an equal quantity of butter, some chopped herbs, and a little bread soaked in milk. Salt and pepper, and fill the white halves with this mixture. Butter a dish and add the remainder of the yolks; place the eggs in the dish, sprinkle with grated bread, pour a little melted butter over them, and put them into a moderate oven for half an hour.

Œufs Brouillés (Eggs).

Warm a lump of butter in a low saucepan. Break the eggs into a bowl, salt and pepper; beat them for a second with a fork; pour them into the melted butter and turn them constantly with a wooden spoon, until they begin to settle into little lumps. The fire must not be too fierce, or the eggs will burn.

Œufs Brouillé au Fromage (Scrambled Eggs and Cheese).

The eggs are scrambled as in the preceding recipe. Just before they are thickening in the saucepan, add about a quarter of a pound of grated cheese to eight or ten eggs.

Œufs Brouillés aux Champignons (Scrambled Eggs and Mushrooms).

Wash some button mushrooms, peel them and chop them into small pieces. Put a lump of butter into a low saucepan; throw in the mushrooms. When they are sufficiently cooked—in about three minutes—add a little more butter if necessary, and the eggs that you will have broken into a bowl, and mix with salt and pepper. Turn all together in the saucepan with a wooden spoon until the eggs thicken. Serve when not too firm.

Amateur cooks sometimes complain that scrambled eggs have a grey unpleasant colour. This curious " grey unpleasant colour " only occurs when the saucepan in which the eggs have been scrambled is not perfectly clean.

Œufs Brouillés aux Pointes d'Asperges (Scrambled Eggs and Asparagus Points).

Cut the hard portion of a small bundle of asparagus from the fresh green points. Put a handful of salt into a saucepan full of hot water. When the water boils bind the bundle of green points together and throw them into the saucepan. After a second or two remove them, cut them into small pieces, and throw them into a low saucepan with a lump of butter; add the eggs prepared for scrambling, with a good pinch of salt and pepper, and turn them together with a wooden spoon until they have sufficiently thickened.

Œufs aux Croûtons (*Eggs and Fried Bread*).

Melt a little butter in a low saucepan; cut a slice of bread into small cubes, throw them into the butter. Pour the eggs into the same saucepan and mix like scrambled eggs.

Œufs à la Neige (*Sweet Snowball Eggs*).

Place a quart of milk in a saucepan on the fire with the rind of a lemon or a little vanilla, and sufficient white sugar to sweeten.

Break six eggs, separating the white from the yolk. Put three tablespoonfuls of powdered white sugar on a plate. Beat the whites of the eggs into a stiff, froth, adding a small pinch of salt. When sufficiently stiff add the sugar and mix briskly. Take a tablespoonful of this mixture and throw it into the boiling milk in the saucepan; turn it three minutes later; remove it with a skimmer and place it on a dish. Take as many spoonfuls of the white of egg as remain and cook them in a similar manner, three or four at a time. (If the white has been beaten sufficiently stiffly, when cooked each spoonful will be a compact mass.) Dress the snowballs in a pyramid on a dish. Pour the remainder of the milk from the saucepan into the yolks of the eggs; put this mixture into another saucepan on the fire, turn it constantly with a spoon, and let it thicken without boiling. Pass it through a strainer, and when cold pour it over the snowballs in the dish.

CHAPTER XIV

To have a palatable dish of macaroni do not select a make of inferior quality. There is only a difference of a penny or so in the price per pound, and it is not really economising to buy the cheaper sort.

Put a saucepan full of water on the fire with a handful of salt. When it boils, break the macaroni into it, in pieces of about a finger-length. Let it boil for twenty minutes, not longer, or the macaroni will become pasty. Strain it, placing the colander on another saucepan or receptacle large enough to hold the water, and pour the contents of the saucepan in which the macaroni has boiled into the colander. Warm a dish, and pour the macaroni into it. Add quickly a lump of butter divided into small pieces, and mix it with the macaroni with a spoon and fork; add also a quarter of a pound of grated Gruyère cheese to half a pound of macaroni. In most cookery books you are told it is essential to mix Parmesan and Gruyère cheeses to have the required flavour, but in the majority of French kitchens excellent dishes of macaroni are prepared with Gruyère cheese alone. Sprinkle a little more salt if necessary, and a little pepper, and serve. The butter and cheese are mixed with the macaroni in the dish, not in the saucepan on the fire.

Macaroni à la Milanaise.

The macaroni is boiled as in the preceding recipe. During the twenty minutes required to bring it to the necessary point, there is ample time to make the sauce that is to season it. Take a couple of ripe tomatoes, wipe them carefully with a fine cloth in order to remove every particle of dust, cut them into halves and place them in a small saucepan with a little butter, two or three onions cut into pieces, a bunch of parsley, thyme, and a bay leaf tied together, a good teaspoonful of salt, and about half that quantity of pepper. Pass this mixture through a strainer when the tomatoes are cooked; put a fresh piece of butter into another small saucepan; add a tablespoonful of flour and incorporate with a wooden spoon; pour in the tomato purée slowly, turning constantly with a spoon; add a little hot water if the sauce is too thick. Turn the macaroni from the saucepan into the colander, and thence on to the dish, and pour the sauce over it, mixing it well so that every piece of the macaroni is coloured red. Serve with grated Gruyère and Parmesan mixed, or with Gruyère alone.

Macaroni à la Crème.

Boil the macaroni as already indicated. Put a small saucepan on the fire with a lump of butter no smaller than an egg; when the butter melts, remove the saucepan to the side and add a tablespoonful of flour, and work one into the other with the indispensable wooden spoon. Moisten with a tumblerful of boiling milk, turning all the time. Let it cook for about ten minutes, whipping it with the egg whisk to prevent the forming of little lumps that may occur with an inexperienced hand. Now add a quarter of a pound of grated Gruyère cheese to the boiling mixture, with a sufficient quantity of salt and pepper to taste; pour the macaroni back again into the saucepan in which it boiled—which is now empty as the water has been strained off—and pour the white sauce upon it. Mix well and serve on a hot dish. For a pound of macaroni the quantities of butter, milk, flour, and cheese must be increased.

Nouilles aux Anchois.

Nouilles are a kind of macaroni made with eggs and eaten as soon as they are prepared. Macaroni, on the other hand, is never eaten quite fresh, and there is no object in doing so, as it contains nothing that will spoil by keeping, although there is a limit to the keeping of macaroni. The nouilles are thrown into a saucepan full of boiling water with a handful of salt. In about a quarter of an hour they are cooked, but it is easy to ascertain at what moment to remove them from the water by tasting if sufficiently soft. While the nouilles are boiling, clean and chop a dozen Gorgona anchovies; put a lump of butter into a small saucepan; and when hot, throw in the anchovies. Pass them through a fine hair sieve. Strain the nouilles and put them on a hot dish, with a quarter of a pound of grated Gruyère cheese to half a pound of nouilles, and a little fresh butter divided into small pieces; mix well with a fork and spoon and pour in the anchovies.

Risotto (Rice à l'Italienne).

Put a handful of salt into a saucepan full of water. Put the saucepan on the fire, and when the water is hot, but not boiling, throw in the rice. Let it boil until the grains are cooked (about twenty minutes). Strain the rice, pouring the contents of the saucepan into a strainer. Put a sufficient quantity of butter into a frying-pan; when the butter is melted, add the rice and mix well together for two or three minutes. Pour the rice into a dish and cover abundantly with grated Parmesan cheese.

Another Risotto (Rice à la Milanaise).

Place a lump of butter into a saucepan; when melted, throw in the rice (about half a pound for four people). Mix rapidly with a wooden spoon to prevent burning. When it begins to colour, moisten with good stock, little by little as required, until the rice is quite cooked—about twenty-five minutes is the time generally calculated, but some qualities of rice require a few minutes more or less. At all events the grains must be intact and not " pappy." Add a teaspoonful of meat extract. Mix with it a couple of pinches of saffron, salt, and pepper, and grated Parmesan cheese. A quarter of a pound of cheese to half a pound of rice is the recognised quantity. A little is mixed with the rice and the remainder served separately, that each guest may take as much or as little as he pleases.

Rice " à la Dreux."

For six people.

Two cupfuls of rice must be washed and strained, placed in a saucepan on the fire, with a lump of butter, and stirred for ten minutes. Then add a little beef extract, with some water, salt and pepper, and cook on a slow fire. When ready, remove the saucepan to the corner of the stove and let the rice dry for half an hour. In the meanwhile chop a couple of kidneys in a little butter, in a frying-pan, with a spoonful of flour and a glass of sherry. When the kidneys are sufficiently cooked, pour the rice into a mould with a hole in the middle, turn it out on a round dish, place scrambled eggs in the hollow, and pour the kidneys with their gravy all over the rice.

An extra word on Rice.

By throwing the rice into hot butter in a pan before adding water to cook it, each grain of rice remains intact.

Gnocchi à l'Italienne.

Ingredients:
One and a half pints of milk.
A little over a quarter of a pound of butter.
Half a pound of semolina.
Five eggs.
Quarter of a pound grated Gruyère cheese.
Two tablespoonfuls of flour.
Salt, pepper, nutmeg.

Pour a pint of milk into a saucepan with a quarter of a pound of butter. When boiling, add the semolina, salt, pepper, and grated nutmeg. Turn it with a wooden spoon until the paste comes away freely from the saucepan. Remove this mixture to the corner of the stove and add the eggs one by one, beating each well into the paste. Then add the greater part of the grated cheese. Stir it well and turn it out on to a board. Cut the paste into small pieces about an inch square. Put a saucepan of hot water on the fire with a handful of salt. When the water boils, throw in the gnocchi or small pieces of paste; let them boil for four minutes; remove them into a strainer, and dip them into cold water. Let them drain. In the meanwhile make a white sauce with butter, flour, and boiling milk (as explained in the chapter on Sauces). Place the gnocchi in a buttered dish, cover them with the sauce, sprinkling them with the remainder of the grated cheese, put them into a quick oven, and serve as soon as they have risen.

Gnocchi with Peas.

Boil the quantity of peas required in plenty of water. In the meanwhile pour a pint of boiling water into a bowl, add five tablespoonfuls of flour, and stir the flour into the water until it becomes a smooth paste. Break the yolks of four eggs, one by one, into the paste, with a little salt. When this mixture is cold it thickens. Then with a teaspoon drop a small portion into the saucepan where the peas are boiling. Continue to drop half a teaspoonful of the paste into the boiling water, and slowly the small pieces will rise to the surface. Let them boil for five or six minutes. Add a pint of hot milk to the peas and paste, and when it has boiled once again pour it into a deep entrée dish or into a soup tureen, as, according to the quantity of liquid, this dish can be eaten as a soup or a vegetarian entrée.

CHAPTER XV

Pouding au Caramel (Bread Pudding).

The simplest of puddings, the most easily made, inexpensive, and excellent, is the bread pudding made by the experienced French cook.

For a quart mould, boil a quart of milk, flavoured with a little lemon peel, just a small quantity cut finely from a lemon. In the meantime break a couple of thick slices of white bread, without the crust, into a basin; add sufficient white sugar to sweeten, and pour the boiling milk over the bread. While this is softening, put the metal mould upon the fire with a little water, and half a dozen lumps of white sugar to make the caramel. This sugar will take a few minutes browning, and during this operation break four eggs into a bowl and beat them well; pass the bread and milk in the basin through a colander with a wooden pestle into another basin; add the eggs, stirring them all the time to mix them well with the bread. Then remove the mould from the fire and shake the brown melted sugar over the sides of the mould, until every part of the interior is covered with a brown coating. Turn the mould quickly and let the cold water from the tap run upon the bottom of it to cool the contents. In a minute the sugar begins to crackle and the caramel is fixed. Now pour the contents of the basin into the mould and bake for half an hour. Let it cool, and empty it on the dish to be served to table. In order to ascertain if the pudding is sufficiently cooked, pass the blade of a knife down the centre. If the knife bears the smallest particle of a smear upon it, the pudding must bake a little longer. It sometimes occurs that a gas fire is used for cooking purposes, then the pudding is coloured under the portion employed for grilling; and when the top is brown, the mould is set into a saucepan of boiling water, and the pudding finishes cooking in what is called a "bain-marie." But the hot oven is the simplest receptacle, and there the pudding is cooked in less time.

Pains Perdus (Entremets).

A favourite dish with old and young, quickly made and appreciated by economical housekeepers.

Cut a number of slices of bread about half an inch thick from a stale loaf; remove the crust and give them all an equal shape, round or square, oval or triangular. As a rule, the square-shaped slices are most practical. Boil a sufficient quantity of milk to soak them, according to the number of slices. Sugar the milk and flavour it with vanilla or lemon, and when cold pour it into a deep dish and add the bread. Let the milk soak well into each slice, then drain on a clean cloth. Beat an egg in a bowl and dip each slice therein, and fry in the following manner: Place a frying-pan on the fire to warm, put into it sufficient butter to cover the surface; when the butter smokes, place the slices of egg-covered bread side by side in the pan, but not close enough to touch; when they are browned on one side, turn them on the other. Sift powdered sugar upon each slice as it is removed from the pan. Dress in a circle, one piece overlapping the other, and fill the interior with jam or marmalade. Serve as hot as possible.

Savarin.

A savarin is one of the typical French sweets that is as common in French households as the British bread pudding. It is made in a special mould, turban-shaped, with a hole in the centre that can be filled with stewed fruit or cream, or fresh strawberries, and is always appreciated.

In a warm utensil place a quarter of a pound of flour. In the centre of this flour add a good teaspoonful of baking powder. Add two eggs. Mix well, cover the paste, and let it rise in a moderate heat for an hour. Then mix therein: butter (the size of an egg) melted, a pinch of salt, and a teaspoonful of powdered sugar. Mix with the hand without beating. Butter the mould, fill it half full, and let it rise until the mould is quite full. Bake in a hot oven for forty minutes.

Make a syrup with a quarter of a pound of sugar and a glass of water. Let it boil a few minutes. When cold, add three or four spoonfuls of rum. When the savarin is cooked, pour the cold syrup over it, with the addition of a little apricot jam.

Soufflé au Chocolat (Chocolate Soufflé).

Three tablets of chocolate, a glass of milk, six whites of eggs, three yolks, a tablespoonful of flour, sugar, salt, and vanilla.

Dissolve the chocolate in a saucepan on a moderate fire, with a little milk, without letting it boil. Mix three spoonfuls of sugar in another saucepan, with the three yolks and a little vanilla. When this mixture becomes smooth like a cream, add the tablespoonful of flour, followed by the milk that has been boiled, the chocolate, and a pinch of salt. Put the saucepan containing these different ingredients upon the fire, and remove it when boiling. Pour it into another vessel in order to cool it, and in the meanwhile beat the whites of the eggs into a stiff froth with a little sugar. Mix the whites carefully with the chocolate mixture when the latter is cold. Butter ever so lightly a soufflé mould, pour the preparation into it until the mould is about half full, to leave space for the soufflé to rise, and put it into the oven for about twenty minutes or more, according to the heat of the oven. In order to judge of the necessary heat to cook a soufflé, try it with a piece of paper, that should brown in the lightest of tints. Serve the soufflé as soon as it has risen and is firm.

Soufflé aux Abricots (Apricot Soufflé).

This is a sweet dish that takes about ten minutes to prepare. Select one pound of ripe apricots of ordinary size, giving about seven to the pound. Peel them, cut them in halves, and mash them with a silver fork, adding a teaspoonful of kirsch. Chop the kernels as fine as possible and mix them with the apricot purée. Beat the white of three fresh eggs to a stiff froth, and gradually add three teaspoonfuls of powdered white sugar. Mix the apricots with the eggs, butter a soufflé dish ever so lightly, pour in the mixture, and put into the oven for about ten minutes. Serve immediately the soufflé is a light brown colour. The oven should not be too hot.

Pudding à la Flory (a Paris Pudding).

Beat the yolks of four eggs with a little over a quarter of a pound of white powdered sugar, a pinch of powdered vanilla, and half a pint of milk. Place this mixture in a saucepan on the fire and let it thicken to a cream, turning it constantly with a wooden spoon, but do not let it boil. Remove it from the fire, and add six leaves of gelatine that have been soaked in cold water. Pour this cream through a fine strainer into a basin, and let it cool. When nearly " set," add a cupful of whipped cream, and pour a little of this mixture into a mould on ice. Add a layer of sponge-cakes (" fingers " if possible) that have soaked in kirsch or rum, and a little preserved fruit cut into cubes, or some fresh strawberries. Cover this with another layer of cream and another of sponge-cake and fruit until the mould is full; add a last layer of cream. When this pudding is quite " set " on ice, turn it out on to a small fringed serviette or d'oyley on a round dish.

Riz Maltais (an Excellent Sweet of Rice and Oranges).

Boil a quarter of a pound of rice with the same quantity of white sugar in a pint of milk with a few strips of the rind of an orange, a small piece of butter, and a pinch of salt. When the rice is well boiled, remove the orange rind, add four leaves of gelatine—previously soaked in a little cold milk—a cupful of double cream, and a couple of drops of cochineal to colour a light pink. Oil a mould with salad oil—not butter, as it is to be iced—decorate it with strips of orange rind, cut as thin as possible, that have boiled a minute or so in water; pour the rice into the mould, let it " set " on ice; then turn it out, and decorate the top with " quarters " of orange soaked in kirsch. Make a sauce with a few spoonfuls of apricot jam in a small cupful of rum. Decorate the rice at the base, when on the dish, with " quarters " of orange steeped in kirsch, one overlapping the other, and pour the sauce around it—not over it.

Pommes Liées (Apples).

Make a syrup with sugar, water, and vanilla; when it boils, throw into the saucepan half a dozen apples, cut into quarters and peeled. In another saucepan boil a pint of milk with three tablespoonfuls of tapioca. When the tapioca and apples are cooked, take a deep dish and pour half the tapioca into it; cover it with a layer of apples, and then add the remainder of the tapioca. Put it into the oven. Make a syrup of apricot jam and the juice from the apples, and pour it over the surface and serve.

Pommes à la Chateaubriand (Apples).

Peel a dozen Canada apples, half-way down only; remove the cores with the usual little instrument without breaking the fruit, and place each apple in a baking-pan in a quick oven. In each cavity put a small piece of butter, a pinch of sugar, and a little white wine or water. Baste them occasionally. When cooked, place them on a dish, and fill each apple with red currant jelly; mix two or three spoonfuls with the juice in the pan, adding a little water if necessary. Pour this sauce over the apples, and serve hot.

Poires à la Condé (Pears and Rice).

Cut some pears into halves, peel them and remove the pips; cook them in a thin syrup with half a stick of vanilla. In the meanwhile boil half a cupful of rice in milk, with a small piece of butter, sugar, and a little vanilla. When the rice is cooked, place it in a border mould, and cover it with a buttered paper. Keep it warm. When ready to serve, turn out the rice on a round dish; arrange the pears in a wreath upon the rice, and pour over them an apricot sauce flavoured with kirsch.

Cerises Victoria (Cherries).

Stone a couple of pounds of cherries. Put half a tumbler of cold water in a saucepan, with a little over half a pound of sugar, on a quick fire. When the sugar has melted, throw in the cherries and let them boil for a few minutes. Mix a dessertspoonful of arrowroot with a little cold water. Add it to the cherries, taking care to shake the saucepan so that the syrup be smooth and equally consistent. Pour the cherries into small silver or china " casseroles " with a little kirsch, brandy, or rum, and set light to them. When the arrowroot is added, the cherries must not boil any longer, they must merely be kept warm as the syrup would be too abundant, and not sufficiently thick. This dish of cherries can also be served in a deep dish and lighted in the same manner when serving.

Gâteau Juliette (Chocolate Cake).

Dissolve four tablets of good chocolate in a little hot water, leaving it very thick. Let it cool, and add four spoonfuls of butter, eight spoonfuls of powdered sugar, two little rolls dried and crushed to powder, eight yolks of eggs, eight whites beaten to a stiff cream. Butter a round mould, pour in the mixture, and put it into the oven for three-quarters of an hour. Turn it out and let it get cold. Cover the cake with a thick layer of marmalade or any sort of jam. Make a sauce of three tablets of chocolate, ten spoonfuls of water, four spoonfuls of sugar. Boil it, turning it constantly with a wooden spoon. Pour the sauce all over the cake, above, beneath, and on all sides.

Chocolate Cake.

For this much-appreciated cake, half a pound of good quality chocolate is required. The remaining ingredients consist of:

A quarter of a pound of sweet almonds with their skin; these must be finely ground.
A quarter of a pound of bitter almonds.
Four eggs, yolks and whites beaten separately.
Half a pound of powdered sugar.
Three spoonfuls of flour.

Melt the chocolate in a little water in a saucepan, on a slow fire. When it thickens, add all the ingredients (with exception of the whites of egg), and beat it all together for ten minutes.

Butter a mould (or even a saucepan), and mix the whites of egg with the paste very lightly. Pour this paste into the buttered mould, and cook slowly on a slow fire. When this cake is slightly coloured, remove it to a piece of paper, then melt a couple of sticks of chocolate in a saucepan with a small piece of butter and a little powdered sugar; this mixture must be very thick, as a layer of it is spread over the cake with a fine brush to make it shiny.

In order to see if it is sufficiently cooked, pierce it with a small stick. This stick should come out somewhat creamy. When successful, the cake weighs heavily. If it is light, it has been too much cooked. This chocolate cake should only be eaten on the following day, and can be kept for a month, if necessary, in an air-tight tin.

Soufflé Rothschild.

This is a sweet dish, said to have been a favourite with King Edward, and always served by the amphitryons who had the honour of receiving him. It is so simple that the ordinary cook can make it, given the necessary care in the quantity and quality of the ingredients. Take eight

7

new-laid eggs; break the yolks into one bowl, the whites
into another. Beat the yolks, adding three tablespoonfuls of powdered sugar, a pinch of salt, and two liqueur
glasses of rum. Beat the whites until they rise to a stiff
froth. Mix one with the other, pouring the whites into
the yolks with a gentle hand; add about half a pound of
candied fruits, cut into small pieces. Pour into a soufflé
dish and bake in a moderate oven for ten minutes. If
possible to procure fresh mulberries, the soufflé Roths-
child is sometimes made with this fruit instead of candied
fruit. The mulberries are mixed intact with the beaten
eggs.

Clafoutis (a Cherry Tart from Limoges).

The ingredients are:
> One pound of flour.
> Four eggs.
> Two spoonfuls of powdered sugar.
> Two liqueur glasses of brandy.
> A pinch of salt.
> A pint of milk.

Sift the flour into a bowl.

Break the eggs, adding salt and sugar; mix well into a
smooth paste.   Then add the milk, and, after removing the
stalks of the cherries (black cherries), throw them into the
paste with the brandy on top.

The receptacle must be well buttered to allow the
" Clafoutis " being easily removed after it has baked in
the oven for about half an hour.   Iced sugar is sprinkled
upon the tart before serving.

A Light Sweet Dish (Lemon Custard Méringue).

For a small pudding to fill the ordinary pie dish sufficient
for six people the ingredients and quantities are:

> Two ounces of potato (two small potatoes or one large).
> Half-pint of milk.
> Two eggs.
> Two lemons.
> A little sugar, a small piece of butter, a dash of vanilla.

Cut the potato into thin slices; put them into a small saucepan on the fire with half the milk. When the potato is cooked, whip it with the remainder until quite smooth. Pour it into the pie dish, or whatever the dish may be that can stand the heat of the oven; add powdered sugar to taste, a little vanilla, a small piece of butter, one grated lemon, and the juice of two; break the yolks of two eggs into the same dish (retaining the whites in another), and stir all together with a fork. Beat each egg into the dish separately. Bake in a slow oven for one hour. Ten minutes before serving whip the whites of the eggs into a stiff froth, adding a little powdered sugar and vanilla. Remove the dish from the oven and cover the contents with these whipped whites. Replace it in the oven, leaving the door open, for about ten minutes, and serve in the same dish with a serviette pinned around it, or encased in a metal dish. This pudding can be made in the lining of a soufflé dish and served in the metal casing. But these details are unimportant; the success of the undertaking from the culinary point of view is the first thing to be studied.

A teaspoonful of desiccated cocoa-nut is an improvement to this pudding, mixed with the ingredients before the whites of the eggs are added.

Beignets de Pommes (Apple Fritters).

For seven or eight people forty or forty-five beignets. Put a little over half a pound of flour (nearly three-quarters of a pound) into a salad bowl, with a pinch of salt. Make a hole in the centre and add the yolks of four eggs (put the whites aside), two tablespoonfuls of salad oil, three of brandy. Mix lightly with a wooden spoon, always in the same direction. Then pour in little by little, turning constantly, a little over half a pint of luke-warm water. When the paste is quite smooth and as thick as cream, after having worked it for about twenty minutes, cover the salad bowl with a cloth and place it near the fire. Peel some good apples (in France the Reinettes are the best for this purpose), remove the pips and cores, and cut them into round slices about the thickness of a penny piece. Just before making the beignets beat the four whites of egg to a froth and add them to the paste in the salad bowl, with a fifth white in order to make it perfect.

Put the frying-pan on the fire with half a pound of lard, and when the steam rises from the pan throw the rounds of apple into the paste and place them one by one (four or five at a time) in the hot lard. When the beignets are a light golden colour turn them on the other side with a fork, and when golden on both sides throw them into a strainer, to strain the fat; powder them with white sugar, and serve as hot as possible.

A Family Cake.

Four eggs. Weigh them and take the same weight in flour, in powdered sugar, and in butter. Break the eggs, separating the whites from the yolks. Mix the powdered sugar with the yolks; add the butter that has been warmed and melted to a paste, the juice of a lemon, and finally the flour. Mix well with a wooden spoon and then beat the whites of the eggs to a stiff froth, and incorporate them with the other ingredients, introducing, however, the whites so carefully that they quite disappear beneath the surface. Then butter a mould, half fill it with this preparation, and bake it in a moderate oven for one hour. The cake must rise to the extent of the mould.

Madeleines.

These little cakes are made with a given quantity of eggs (four, six, eight, according to the number of cakes required) and the weight of the eggs in flour, sugar, and butter. They are mixed with a wooden spoon in the same way as in the " Family Cake," but the whites of the eggs are added at the same time as the yolks without any further preparation. Special moulds are used for madeleines with small indented lines. Each mould is filled with the paste, and baked for three-quarters of an hour in a moderately heated oven. A pinch of salt is added to the mixture of eggs, butter, sugar, and flour.

ICES

The making of ices is one of the simplest of operations, given an ice machine. And as the ordinary ice pudding is not an expensive affair, it will be found interesting to follow exactly the methods in use in French families, where the cook is merely the homely person who assists in the housework.

Vanilla Ice.

Half a pound of sugar. Six yolks of eggs. One stick of vanilla. One quart of milk.

Put the milk, sugar, and vanilla into a saucepan on the fire. When boiling, pour it on to the yolks that have been beaten in a bowl, mixing them quickly with a wooden spoon. Pass this mixture through a hair sieve and let it cool. Three hours before serving, pour this custard into the centre of the ice machine, and surround it with six or eight pounds of rough ice broken into fine pieces, and two pounds of coarse salt. Turn the handle for about half an hour, until the ice " sets." Then take it out with a spoon and put it into a mould. Cover the mould with buttered paper before affixing the cover, and put the mould into the machine again.

It is easy to know when the ice is " setting," as the handle becomes more and more difficult to work. Turn the ice in the mould on to a round dish upon a napkin or a fancy d'oyley.

Coffee Ice.

The same as the vanilla ice, without the vanilla. In its place a little essence of coffee.

Chocolate Ice.

The same as the vanilla ice, but instead of vanilla dissolve eight tablets of chocolate in a little water, which you add to the mixture of eggs, milk, and sugar before passing it through the sieve.

Bombe Printanière.

Make a vanilla ice in the manner indicated; add, just before putting it into the mould, candied fruits chopped fine, that have been impregnated with kirsch.

Bombe Marquise.

Make a vanilla ice and put it into a mould. Grate a little chocolate, and just before serving remove a portion with a spoon and fill the vacuum with the grated chocolate.

Soufflé Surprise.

A sure success at a dinner-party, the soufflé surprise is one of the least complicated of dishes. It requires a light hand and plenty of courage. Why? Simply because this " sweet " is composed of ice and eggs, and the ice covered with the eggs is put into a hot oven. Here is the recipe, and if carefully followed there is no possibility of a failure. For a party of six or eight place a low-shaped vanilla ice in a silver entrée dish, in the centre. Break six eggs, keeping the yolks and whites separate. Sweeten the yolks and flavour with vanilla; beat them for a few minutes, until well mixed one with the other; beat the whites into a stiff froth. Mix the yolks and whites lightly together and pour them over the ice, masking the entire dish. Let the oven be red-hot. Take your courage in your two hands (as the French say), and slip the dish into the oven. In a few minutes, the time necessary to make an omelette soufflé, the eggs rise and brown ever so slightly, and the ice does not melt. Serve immediately with hot plates. This injunction is essential, as the soufflé must not cool, or the opposition of hot and cold would be decreased, and in a measure lost. If the party consist of ten or twelve people, it is advisable to make two soufflés surprises, instead of increasing the number of eggs. The ice must be made very firm, and in a low mould, no higher than a breakfast cup.

Glace aux Fraises (Strawberry Ice).

A little over half a pound of sugar.
One quart of water.
One and a half pounds of strawberries; the juice of two
lemons.

Dissolve the sugar in the water in an earthenware
saucepan.   Squeeze the lemons therein, and strain through
the hair sieve.   Pass the strawberries through a fine sieve,
and mix them with the syrup.   Colour with a little cochineal.   Proceed in the same manner as for the vanilla ice.

Raspberry Ice.

The same as for the strawberry ice, but without the
lemon.

Another Word on Ices.

Vanilla ice is sometimes served with hot chocolate
poured over it.

CHAPTER XVI

Evening Meals—Vegetarian Diet.

The French doctors are advocating one meat meal a day, partaken of at midday, and in many households it has become a general thing to dine at night on the lightest possible food, preparing and serving a vegetarian diet as coquettishly as if it were a menu of the most luxurious viands. The dinner consists of courses in the usual way, and the cook takes pains to make the dish of peas, rice, eggs, etc., as appetising in aspect and taste as possible. In the ordinary French middle-class family, where the same food is prepared for the kitchen as for the family, the non-meat meal is not a subject of complaint, as it might be in England, for with the wisdom that comes from experience French servants always abstain from meat at night. They will tell you—if you ask them— that they are healthier and more able to work without it; and as we are gradually coming back to the land we acknowledge that the peasants' notions of hygienic food are the right ones, the natural ones, springing from their early education in the fields and farms.

For the summer, heavy meals, supposed to be indispensable to a well-ordered dinner, are barbarisms. If you will try the effect of a summer dinner without fish, fowl, or meat, invite your friends to partake of the following menu. Prepare them for a Parisian repast and note how they will enjoy it, and how many men in their middle age will be grateful for the palatable manner in which they can prevent the hardening of their arteries, lengthening their lives by avoiding eating so much meat.

A SUMMER EVENING MENU

Meon (Cantaloup)
Soufflé au Fromage
Haricots à la Crème
Œufs en Gelée Salade
Riz Impératrice aux Fraises
Fruits de Saison

MENUS FOR THE WEEK

Macaroni
Peas à la Française
Lettuce Salad with hard Eggs
Stewed Strawberries and Cherries
Fresh Cream

Sorrel Soup
Gnocchi with Peas
Cos Lettuce Salad
Boiled Custards
Stewed Fruit

Risotto (Rice with Tomato Sauce)
French Beans Sautés
Water-cress Salad
Caramel Cream
Fruit

Spring Soup
Spinach with Poached Eggs
Potato Croquettes
Salad
Stewed Fruit

Macaroni with White Sauce
Macédoine of Vegetables
Tomato Salad
Stewed Fruit

Vermicelli and Sorrel Soup
Artichokes with Butter Sauce
Stewed Lettuces
Potato Salad
Macédoine of Fruits

Vegetable Soup
Carrots with a White Sauce
Salad with Hard Eggs
Stewed Fruit

CHAPTER XVII

HOW TO MAKE COFFEE

How is it that England has such a bad reputation for making coffee? The coffees imported into the United Kingdom are of first-rate quality, yet the decoction served there, after luncheon and dinner, in the majority of houses, is detestable. To what can this be attributed?

Simply to the fact that the ordinary housekeeper buys coffee that has not only been *roasted*, but *ground*, thereby losing strength and flavour.

I allow that it is not always convenient to roast coffee at home, although there is nothing less complicated—given the machines to be found at any ironmonger's. But to buy coffee ground by the grocer is one of the primary causes of the inferiority of English-made coffee. Let me therefore impress upon those averse from " roasting " the necessity of buying their coffee in the bean, procuring it as freshly roasted as possible.

The beans should be kept in an earthen or china vessel, hermetically closed, not—as is generally the case—in tins; and ground in the ordinary little mill, just at the moment required.

Café Noir (Black Coffee).

For every small cup, take one tablespoonful of ground coffee.

Measure the water, allowing one cupful per person, and a little over that will be absorbed by the coffee.

Make it in the ordinary earthenware or metal percolating pot. Scald the lower receptacle as for tea-making.

Place the coffee upon the percolator. Pour, little by little, boiling water in the measured quantity, and let it stand until it has filtered through the coffee. Serve as hot as possible.

It goes without saying that the better the quality the better the cup of coffee. It is a mistake to imagine that a mixture of coffees brings out the aroma. This is an exploded theory.

Café-au-lait (Coffee with Milk).

Whilst in black coffee not a particle of chicory is added, the secret of *café-au-lait*—as the French understand it— lies in the addition of one spoonful of chicory for every two spoonfuls of ground coffee.

For a breakfast cupful of *café-au-lait* take the same quantity of coffee and the same quantity of water as for a small cup of black coffee. When the coffee is made, add two-thirds of boiling milk to one-third of coffee. In other words: one-third of the breakfast cup consists of coffee and two-thirds of milk.

In order to extract the full essence from the beans, some cooks pour boiling water over the grounds that remain in the percolator, and make use of this, instead of ordinary water, for preparing the coffee the next day. Experts, however, contend that perfection is reached when the water boils but once; it is therefore only for coffee which will be mixed with milk (*café-au-lait*) that this process of extracting the remaining essence from the grounds can be recommended.

CHAPTER XVIII

COOKING WITHOUT EGGS

A Rice Pudding without Eggs or Sugar

A pint of milk, a small coffee cupful of rice, the same quantity of dried figs, a little lemon juice.

Put the milk, the rice, and lemon juice in a saucepan on the fire; simmer for thirty or forty minutes. Cook the figs in a little water, and add them to the rice. Sugar a mould and pour in the preparation. Put the mould of rice in the oven and turn out when cooled.

A Sweet with neither Butter, Milk, nor Eggs.

One pound of potatoes boiled in their skins, flour, a little sugar and grated lemon peel.

Mash the potatoes and pass them through a sieve, mix them with grated lemon or orange peel and sufficient flour to make a smooth paste. Knead this paste on a board, roll it, and cut it in rounds with a wineglass. Throw these rounds into hot dripping in the pan, and when brown on each side serve them covered with powdered sugar.

Mayonnaise without Eggs.

With the remains of a white sauce (béchamel) an excellent mayonnaise is made by adding oil, drop by drop, stirring continually. This is completed with a little salt, pepper, and a spoonful of mustard.

Chocolate Cream without Eggs.

A pint of milk, butter (the size of an egg), a little sugar, the same weight in cocoa, with a little cold milk or water.

Pour this mixture into the boiling milk, stir it and let it simmer for ten minutes. Add the butter just before serving.

Pancakes without Eggs.

Mix two teaspoonfuls of baking powder with a cup of flour and half a teaspoonful of salt, add milk and water sufficient to make a paste, and a tablespoonful of melted butter.

Place a little salad oil and butter in a pan, and heat. When sufficiently hot, drop a spoonful of the paste therein, and, when it bubbles, turn on the other side. Put on a warm dish and serve hot. This quantity makes nine small pancakes.

Scones.

Make the same paste as for the pancakes, add a lump of butter, mix well into the flour, then the milk and water. Heat oil and butter in the pan; roll the paste, and cut in rounds or squares, and fry.

An Alsatian Omelette with Few Eggs.

The Alsatian omelette is worth recording. In Alsace the evening meal consists generally of a soup, an omelette, and a salad. Here is the recipe for the omelette.

For each person: one egg, two tablespoonfuls of flour, a little milk, and a pinch of salt.

Start by putting the flour in a bowl, with the salt and some of the milk. Add the yolk of the egg and the white beaten to a froth. Place a little fat or oil in a pan on the fire, drop therein the preparation that should spread like a big pancake. When cooked on one side, turn it, let it colour, and serve.

This omelette is excellent and very nourishing. In summer when milk has " turned " it can be used for this purpose.

It can also be cut in pieces and served in the gravy of the meat. This is little known and will be found good.

A third way is to put the pieces in a dish and serve them with any sauce without meat.

This omelette can also be made with two potatoes instead of flour, and a handful of Gruyère cheese.

A Bread Omelette.

Dry bread, sufficient to be moistened by half a glass of milk, one egg, salt and pepper, and a little grated cheese are required.

A spoonful of dripping is put into the pan, the bread and milk are warmed and cooled, the yolk of the egg added to the white beaten to a froth. The dripping is heated and the preparation thrown in and cooked like a pancake.

Roasts without Meat.

These recipes contain the same quantity of albumin as meat, fish or fowl, without one or the other, and, in fact, have a greater nutritive value.

1. One egg, the same weight in bread, half a glass of milk, a handful of grated Gruyère cheese, a carrot, salt, pepper, a sprig of thyme, and a bay leaf. Make a paste of bread soaked in milk, the yolk of an egg, the Gruyère, salt and pepper, and the white of egg whipped to a stiff froth. Make a sausage of these ingredients in what is called in France a " crépinette " (bought at the pork butcher's). Brown this sausage in fat of some description or other, on all sides, and place it with the fat (in which it has browned) in a saucepan, with an onion and a carrot, and let it simmer until cooked.

2. Half a pound of rice, two eggs, a handful of grated Gruyère cheese, a glass of milk, butter or margarine the size of an egg.

Heat the butter or margarine, throw in the rice (that has been washed), let it colour slightly, add the milk and a little water, salt, and cook for half an hour. Break the eggs, beat them well, and add the cheese. Remove the saucepan from the fire, let the contents cool, and add the eggs and Gruyère.

Butter a mould and sprinkle grated bread thereon, pour in the preparation, bake for thirty minutes in the oven, and then place the mould in a " bain-marie " (hot water in a saucepan) and cook for an hour. Turn out of the mould and serve.

3. One pound of lentils or beans, two spoonfuls of tomato purée, a sprinkling of grated Gruyère, two eggs, an onion, a carrot and a turnip, thyme and bay leaf, salt and pepper.

Soak the beans or lentils for twelve hours, place them covered with water in a saucepan on the fire, with the herbs and vegetables, salt and pepper. Let them simmer for four hours. Break the eggs, add the Gruyère, mix well, and pour into the lentils or beans when the latter have cooled. Pour this preparation into a mould lined with " *crépinette*," bake for thirty minutes, turn it out and serve with or without a tomato sauce.

The same preparation can be made with a pound of potatoes instead of lentils or beans; or, instead of potatoes, a pound of chestnuts.

A Cake made with Lentils or Beans.

Make a purée of a pound of lentils or beans. Add half a pound of dried figs, two pieces of sugar, and a little vanilla. Cut the figs in small pieces, cook them with the vanilla, mix them with the purée, pour into a sugared mould, turn out and serve cold.

A Cake of Dried Vegetables and Nuts.

One pound of lentils or beans, two eggs, a handful of shelled almonds or walnuts, half a glass of milk, a little soaked bread, and a quarter of a pound of figs.

Make a paste of the bread and vegetables, add the eggs well beaten, and the nuts (that must be pounded); butter and sugar a mould, throw in the preparation, and bake for thirty minutes.

CHAPTER XIX

MENUS

WITH RECIPES FROM THE BEST PARIS CHEFS

IT is as difficult to make a menu as a programme for a piano recital, and there are dinners as heavy as concerts. In order, therefore, to avoid failure in compiling a menu, here are a few examples of dinners served at some of the famous Paris restaurants, and these may serve as types for all occasions when a ceremonious menu is required.

Menu. (*Ledoyen.*)

Crème d'Écrevisse
Consommé Marie Stuart
Truite Saumonée à la Royale
Noisette de Présalé aux Primeurs
Suprême de Caneton Demidoff
Granité au Porto Doré
Poularde Ledoyen
Cailles en Chaudfroid
Asperges Sauce Mousseline
Glace Opéra
Fruits   Dessert

(Dinner offered by the Duc Decazes after the automobile boat race at Toulon.)

Recipes from the Chef.

TRUITE SAUMONÉE A LA ROYALE

The trout is poached in sauterne, the skin is removed when the fish is cooked, and the pink flesh lies blushingly on a dish surrounded with bouquets of truffles, quenelles, and crayfish. It is served with a port sauce.

POULARDE LEDOYEN

This is a capon abundantly truffled; but a truffled capon is not a Poularde Ledoyen. Besides the truffles it is stuffed with foie gras. This highly seasoned bird is served with a timbale of truffles cooked in champagne.

Menu.   (*Café de la Paix.*)

Huîtres Colchester
Hors-d'œuvre
Homard à l'Écossaise
Noisette d'Agneau Henri IV.
Ailerons de Poussins Savoyarde
Suprême de Canetons à la Paix
Salade Parisienne
Glace Opéra   Dessert

Recipes.

HOMARD À L'ÉCOSSAISE

This is a lobster served hot, and more appetisingly dressed than the majority of its kind. The instructions are to cut a large lobster into pieces while still alive, season with salt and cayenne, and brown on both sides in a low stewing-pan in a mixture of oil and butter. When coloured to a golden brown, add a lump of butter and a spoonful of tomatoes in purée (tomato sauce). Cover the saucepan and let the lobster cook for a quarter of an hour. Then remove the flesh from the shell and place it in a soufflé dish. Pass the sauce remaining in the saucepan through a sieve, let it boil for a few minutes without a cover, to reduce it, and thicken with a cupful of cream and a glass of Scotch whisky. Serve as hot as possible.

NOISETTE DE PRÉSALÉ HENRI IV.

This is the equivalent of the English Southdown mutton. Take the fleshiest part of chops for as many as there are guests, and brown them in butter. When well cooked, place them on rounds of fried bread. Reduce the sauce in the frying-pan with a small glass of sherry and some good meat extract. Cover the noisettes with the sauce and serve at the same time a béarnaise in a sauce-boat and a dish of potato croquettes.

AILERONS DE POUSSINS SAVOYARDE

Take the wings of very young chickens, salt them, colour them in butter, clarify, and cover the saucepan. Let them cook for fifteen minutes. In the meanwhile prepare a few small potatoes, mushrooms, artichokes in quarters, small onions, and a little lean bacon; colour them in butter, and add them to the chicken in the saucepan.

The wings or ailerons (which should be now ready) are placed in the centre of a dish, and the above garnish placed around them in little heaps. Put half a tumbler of white wine and a little strong stock into the saucepan where the chickens have cooked, add salt and pepper to taste, and pour it over the dish with a pinch of chopped parsley.

SALADE PARISIENNE

This is a wonderful salad, composed of potatoes cut into cubes, peas, asparagus points, artichoke fonds, small carrots, celery root, French beans and flageolets. Season with a mayonnaise, to which you add a little meat jelly and a glass of good brandy. Decorate the top of the salad with slices of truffles, asparagus points, and bouquets of cauliflower.

SUPRÊME DE CANETONS " À LA PAIX "

A famous dish of duck that seems to have taken the place of the pressed duck—once so fashionable. The duck is roasted, and stuffed when cold with foie gras, cream, and a glass of port; the fillets are cut and placed side by side upon the carcase, as usual. This is a great supper dish.

Menu. (*Ritz.*)

Caviar Blinis
Tortue Claire
Filets de Sole Alexandre
Poularde Washington
Purée Favorite
Pommes Macaire
Bécasses au Frémet
Salade
Asperges Vertes
Poires Duchesse de Devonshire
Corbeilles de Fruits

Recipes.

CAVIAR BLINIS

Small pancakes of black corn served with caviar.

FILETS DE SOLE ALEXANDRE

Remove the fillets from a large sole, flatten and roll them, poach them in a good bouillon (made with the bones, head, and tail of the fish, a few slices of onions, herbs, and a dash of vinegar). Stuff them with quenelles of crayfish, cooked in the same bouillon as the fillets of sole.

Make a thick béchamel sauce and let it cool. When cold cut in a diamond pattern, thick enough to hold one of the fillets when the interior of the béchamel is scooped out. Remove the top of the shaped béchamel very carefully, in order to replace it upon the part that contains the fish. Cover with bread-crumbs and vermicelli, and fry in butter. Serve with a chablis sauce.

POULARDE WASHINGTON

Select a large capon. About a dozen heads of maize corn are boiled and taken from the husk, lightly coloured in butter, mixed with a spoonful of suprême sauce, and used as a stuffing for the bird. Forty to fifty minutes must be allowed to cook the capon in a deep pan, in a moderate oven. The capon is then placed on a hot dish, and a glass of whisky, half a pint of cream, a little beef extract, and a pinch of cayenne are stirred into the pan to make the sauce. If fresh maize is not obtainable, tinned maize can be used.

PURÉE FAVORITE

Boil two pounds of French beans in salted water, until quite tender. Make them into a purée, mix with cream (a small cupful). Salt and pepper.

Menus 117

Menu. (*Foyot.*)

Crème Windsor—Ox Tail
Barquettes d'Écrevisses Nantua
Truite Saumonée au Vin Chambertin
Baron d'Agneau de Pouillac aux Morilles
Salmis de Gelinottes au Xérès
Foie Gras Frais à la Souvaroff
Sorbet au Kummel
Canard à l'Archiduc—Poularde Truffée
Salade Monselet
Asperges d'Argenteuil Sauce Mousseline
Petits Pois Nouveaux à la Française
Timbales de Fruits Glacés à l'Orange
Glace Viviane
Feuilleté aux Amandes
Dessert

(Dinner served at the Élysée Palace to H.M. King Edward in May, 1905.)

Recipes.

SALADE MONSELET

Take a large head of celery and cut it into small pieces —as small as possible—the hearts of two endives (chicory) cut in the same manner, a dozen peeled walnuts, broken into pieces. Season with a mayonnaise, and garnish at the summit with fillets of anchovies and olives. These quantities are sufficient for six people moderately fond of salad. For immoderate salad-eaters it must be reckoned for two.

Menu. (*Café Riche.*)

Caviar
Consommé Riche
Sole Giselle
Ris de Veau Belgrand
Médaillon
Suprême de Behague Favorite
Foie Gras Bonnaure
Salade Ninette
Soufflé Jaffa
Fruits   Dessert

Recipes from the Chef.

CONSOMMÉ RICHE

A soup made with the ordinary ingredients of a strong bouillon, thickened with tomatoes, celery, and artichokes in purées.

SOLE GISELLE

A sole cooked in white wine flavoured with asparagus points and shrimps.

HOMARD DORIA

A variation of the Homard à l'Américaine—lobster cut into pieces and served hot—with truffles and mushrooms added to a béchamel sauce thickened to a cream with grated Gruyère cheese.

SUPRÊME DE BEHAGUE FAVORITE

Fillets of venison cooked in butter and Bordeaux, served on a purée of French beans.

POULET POCHÉ FORESTIÈRE

Chicken prepared in a frying-pan, surrounded with mushrooms à la crème; in plain English, the button species of mushrooms in a béchamel sauce.

MÉDAILLON À LA RICHE

Fillets of beef with Madeira, truffles, and small balls of potatoes.

CANETON DE ROUEN À LA FRANÇAISE

Roast duckling, with the sauce made with the duck's liver mashed with the gravy, and a glass of brandy.

TERRINE DE FOIE GRAS BONNAURE

Foie gras served in a port jelly.

Salade Ninette

A salad composed of finely sliced celery, asparagus points, tomatoes, and truffles; the celery and tomatoes are raw, the dressing made of cream, vinegar, salt, pepper, and mustard. The cream takes the place of oil and gives a more delicate flavour.

Soufflé Jaffa

Vanilla ice served in an orange.

Pêches Thaïs

Poached peaches, with a purée of strawberries and fresh almonds covering a vanilla ice inserted in the fruit, in the place of the stone. The fruit is cut into halves, the ice inserted, and covered with the purée.

Recipes given by the Chef at Marguery's.

Sole Marguery (Sole Normande)

Fillet the soles and lay them in a flat pan. Moisten them with a glass of white wine, and season with salt and pepper. When the fillets are cooked, remove them to a dish and reduce the contents of the pan. Add to this " reduction " one or two yolks of eggs, according to the quantity of fish. Let them thicken to a cream on a moderate fire, and add little by little a good-sized piece of butter, taking care that the sauce is never more than warm. Throw in some chopped parsley. Garnish the fillets with peeled shrimps and mussels, and pour the sauce over all. Put the dish in a hot oven for four minutes and serve.

Tournedos Chasseur

Cut as many thick slices of fillet of beef as there are guests. Give them the shape of a five-franc piece. Put some butter into a low saucepan with the fillets, let them colour on both sides on a quick fire. When cooked, take them from the saucepan and throw into the gravy a good pinch of chopped shalots. Moisten with a little white wine and the same quantity of sherry, a spoonful of tomato sauce, and a little concentrated bouillon. Add chopped parsley and tarragon, and pour the sauce over the tournedos. The meat must not boil with the sauce.

HOMARD À L'AMÉRICAINE

This particular method of preparing lobsters is almost as celebrated as the sole. Cut two or three onions and carrots into cubes. Add a bay leaf and a pinch of thyme. Cook them in butter in a saucepan large enough to hold the lobster, which must be cut up alive into small pieces. Moisten with a glass of sherry, two glasses of white wine, and a fresh tomato reduced to pulp. Cover the saucepan hermetically. Cook on a quick fire for a quarter of an hour. Season with pepper and salt and a dash of cayenne; add a piece of butter the size of an egg, before serving.

POULET À LA PARMENTIER

Cut a fowl into the ordinary pieces. Place them in a saucepan with a lump of butter. Pepper and salt. Let them colour on both sides very slowly for about ten minutes, add potatoes (peeled) and a few small onions. Cover the saucepan hermetically and let the contents stew on a slow fire.

Add a sprinkling of chopped parsley when ready for serving.

Menu (Luncheon). (*Tour d'Argent.*)

Œufs Claude Lowther
Filet de Sole Bertron
Escalopes de Ris de Veau Bénet
Caneton Tour d'Argent
Salade Roger
Fonds d'Artichauts au Fondu
Fruits Glacés
Café   Liqueurs

Recipes.

ŒUFS CLAUDE LOWTHER

The aspect of the eggs à la Claude Lowther is much the same as of ordinary scrambled eggs with asparagus points, but there is a delicacy in the flavour that has nothing ordinary about it. Instead of mixing the eggs with milk in the orthodox fashion, take thick cream, add the asparagus points at the last moment and season well.

FILET DE SOLE BERTRON

The fillet is served in the shell of the crayfish; the interior of the little écrevisse in the sauce.

ESCALOPES DE RIS DE VEAU BÉNET

Sweetbreads with a good creamy béchamel sauce, mixed with truffles and morils (yellow mushrooms).

FONDS D'ARTICHAUTS AU FONDU

This is a delightful dish, and much less complicated than it looks. Make a cheese soufflé in the usual way. Boil the artichokes, remove the leaves, and into each fond pour a sufficient quantity of the soufflé mixture to cover it. Bake for fifteen minutes in the oven, and serve on a hot dish.

Menu. (*Lapérouse.*)

Crème d'Écrevisses
Printanier aux Quenelles
Hors-d'œuvre Variés
Filet de Sole Lapérouse
Aloyau Braisé à la Lucullus
Petits poulets pochés aux pointes d'asperges
Cèpes Bordelaises
Petits Pois Paysanne
Canard Farci
Salade Italienne
Soufflé Palmyre
Fruits   Dessert

(Dinner served to the new Prix de Rome.)

Recipes by the Chef.

FILETS DE SOLE LAPÉROUSE

The soles are filleted and poached in a good fish stock. Mussels, shrimps, and mushrooms garnish the dish when the soles are ready to be served, and a béchamel sauce is poured over them.

SOUFFLÉ PALMYRE

A soufflé is made in the ordinary way with butter, flour, milk, sugar, and the yolks of six eggs—the whites beaten to a stiff froth and added when the soufflé mixture is cold. Two or three sponge-cakes are cut into small pieces and steeped in aniseed. These are poured into the soufflé, which is then covered with grated macaroons. After remaining five minutes in a hot oven, the soufflé is powdered with white sugar and replaced in the oven for a quarter of an hour.

Recipes given by the Chef at Champeaux.

SOLE À LA CHAMPEAUX

Poach the sole with a little stock and some good white wine. When cooked, add a little pepper and reduce the sauce. Thicken with the yolks of two eggs and a lump of butter. The better the quality of the butter the more delicate is the sauce. Pass the sauce through a fine sieve. Sprinkle a few peeled shrimps on the sole, pour the sauce over it, cover lightly with grated bread-crumbs, and put it into a hot oven for five minutes. Serve with écrevisses.

LAITANCE DE CARPE EN CAISSE

Poach some roes in white wine and stock, add mushrooms, thyme, bay leaf, onions, and butter to flavour. Reduce the sauce and thicken with two or three yolks of eggs and a little fresh butter. Butter some paper cases, colour them in the oven, strain the roes on a napkin, place them in the cases and cover them with the sauce.

POULET À LA HELDER

Cut a chicken into halves, without quite separating it. Season with salt and pepper and place it in a low saucepan with a good-sized lump of butter. Cover it hermetically and let it cook in the oven, basting it occasionally with the butter. When the chicken is nearly ready, add two table-spoonfuls of good stock.

Poulet à la Champeaux

Cut a chicken into ordinary pieces, colour them in butter; when a golden brown add chopped parsley, moisten with white wine, a glass of sherry, a little strong gravy, and let them finish cooking in a covered saucepan. Place them in an entrée dish, add fresh butter to the sauce and pour it over. Boil in another saucepan some small round potatoes. Colour them in hot butter. Prepare some small onions in the same way, and serve them in alternate heaps round the chicken.

Pouding Diplomate

Make a cream composed of the yolks of four eggs, powdered sugar, milk, and gelatine. Let it cool, and add a cupful of whipped cream, four sponge-cakes cut into pieces, and some mixed candied fruits in cubes, a glass of kirsch, and a glass of maraschino. Mix well and turn it into a fancy mould. Surround it with ice, and in half an hour it is ready to be served.

Menu. (*Durand.*)

Hors-d'œuvre Variés
Consommé Portugais
Barbue à la Durand
Ris de Veau Régence
Pièce de Bœuf Braisée Favorite
Ortolans sur Croustades
Salade de Saison
Asperges Sauce Mousseline
Bombe Victoria
Dessert

(Dinner offered by the Marquise de Jancourt to King Edward on his last visit to Paris as Prince of Wales.)

Recipes by the Chef.

Sole Durand

Place the sole, which at Durand's, as in all first-class kitchens, is always skinned on both sides, in a stew-pan that has been well buttered. Season with salt and pepper, add a tablespoonful of tomato sauce, a sprig of thyme, a bay leaf, chopped parsley, a little white wine, and some fish stock. Cover it and let it cook in the oven. When quite " done," remove the sole into a hot dish, strain the sauce, add a lump of butter and cream to thicken it, and the juice of a lemon. Pour the sauce over the sole and serve hot.

SALADE DURAND

Cut into thin strips several boiled potatoes according to the quantity of salad required. Add truffles, fonds of artichokes, asparagus points, celery (also cut into strips); place them in an ice timbale. Season with a mayonnaise.

POULET DURAND

This is a very simple and excellent recipe for an entrée of chicken. For eight people take two chickens, carve them, and cook in butter, pepper and salt, turning them on both sides to colour. They can be browned either in the oven or in a sauté-pan on a moderate fire. In the meanwhile make a purée of artichokes, using the fonds of a dozen; add a good béchamel to the purée and place it in the centre of the dish, surrounded by the pieces of chicken. A small bunch of asparagus points surmount the purée like a flag. Sometimes the purée is ornamented with carrots, turnips, and potatoes cut into tiny balls, and cooked in butter; but the simple purée satisfies epicures.

Menu. (Luncheon). (*Voisin.*)
Hors-d'œuvre Variés
Sole Grillée Rouvier
Entrecote Sauce Bordelaise
Ortolan à la Caprille
Petits Pois à la Française
Parfait au Café
Fromage   Dessert

Recipes by the Chef.

ENTRECÔTE SAUCE BORDELAISE

This must not be mistaken for the entrecôta " à la Bordelaise." The latter is a steak cooked on the grill, which, as soon as the side that is " cooked " is turned, is sprinkled with chopped shalot and parsley; and when the steak is in the dish, butter, salt, pepper, and a dash of lemon are added. The entrecôte " Sauce Bordelaise " is served with small rounds of marrow and a red wine sauce. The marrow bone should be placed in cold water for twenty-four hours if possible, the water changed several times, as the marrow is then whiter and more appetising; otherwise it is always more or less grey. Put the bone into a saucepan full of cold water without salt. When the water boils, remove the saucepan to the side of the fire, to remain hot without boiling. Cover it and let the marrow poach for five-and-twenty or thirty minutes. It is shaken from the bone and cut into slices when the entrecôte is ready to be served.

For the sauce, put a tumblerful of claret, half that quantity of very good stock, and a pinch of sugar into a small saucepan. Boil without covering it, until it is reduced by half. Add chopped shalot and a small bay leaf; boil for five or six minutes; pass the sauce through a fine sieve, and add the juice of a lemon, salt, pepper, a little cayenne, and a lump of butter.

The entrecôte is carved, salted and peppered, and the pieces placed one next the other in the original shape; the slices of marrow are cut with a warm knife and arranged in the centre the length of the steak, and the sauce is poured lightly over.

Ortolan à la Caprille

Stuff a plump ortolan with truffles. Moisten with Madeira and place in the shell of a turkey's egg, carefully washed and slightly greased with the purest of olive oil. This shell is placed in burning cinders with nothing but the head of the bird peeping from the top. Here in the shell the ortolan melts, little by little, like a lump of butter; the fat rises to the surface, is removed with a teaspoon and replaced with a few drops of Alicante. When the bird is cooked, there is nothing more delicate, more delicious, more original than the Ortolan à la Caprille.

SPECIAL INDEX

This Special Index contains a number of recipes conveniently classified under six different headings. It is given so that the busy housewife can discover readily new and tasty dishes suited to particular occasions or purposes.

PRINTED IN GREAT BRITAIN BY BILLING AND SONS, LTD., GUILDFORD AND ESHER